D1033542

# PATHWAYS

## Listening, Speaking, and Critical Thinking

# 4B

Paul MacIntyre

 NATIONAL GEOGRAPHIC LEARNING |  CENGAGE Learning

Andover • Melbourne • Mexico City • Stamford, CT • Toronto • Hong Kong • New Delhi • Seoul • Singapore • Tokyo

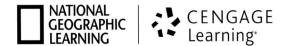

**Pathways Split Text 4B**
**Listening, Speaking, and Critical Thinking**
Paul MacIntyre

Regional Director, Asia ELT/School:
Michael Cahill

Publisher, Asia ELT/School: Edward Yoshioka

Regional Manager, Production & Rights (Asia):
Pauline Lim

Senior Production Executive (Asia): Cindy Chai

Publisher: Sherrise Roehr

Executive Editor: Laura Le Dréan

Acquisitions Editor: Tom Jefferies

Associate Development Editor:
Marissa Petrarca

Director of Global Marketing: Ian Martin

Marketing Manager: Caitlin Driscoll

Marketing Manager: Katie Kelley

Marketing Manager: Emily Stewart

Director of Content and Media Production:
Michael Burggren

Content Project Manager: Daisy Sosa

Manufacturing Manager: Marcia Locke

Manufacturing Buyer: Marybeth Hennebury

Cover Design: Page 2 LLC

Cover Image: JIM BRANDENBURG/MINDEN
PICTURES/National Geographic Image
Collection

Interior Design: Page 2 LLC

Composition: Cenveo Publisher Services/
Nesbitt Graphics, Inc.

© 2013 National Geographic Learning, a part of Cengage Learning

ALL RIGHTS RESERVED. No part of this work covered by the copyright herein may be reproduced, transmitted, stored or used in any form or by any means graphic, electronic, or mechanical, including but not limited to photocopying, recording, scanning, digitizing, taping, Web distribution, information networks, or information storage and retrieval systems, except as permitted under Section 107 or 108 of the 1976 United States Copyright Act, without the prior written permission of the publisher.

For product information and technology assistance, contact us at
**Cengage Learning Asia Customer Support, 65-6410-1200**

For permission to use material from this text or product,
submit all requests online at **www.cengageasia.com/permissions**
Further permissions questions can be emailed to
**asia.permissionrequest@cengage.com**

ISBN 13: 978-1-285-15979-9
ISBN 10: 1-285-15979-9

**Cengage Learning Asia Pte Ltd**
151 Lorong Chuan #02-08
New Tech Park
Singapore 556741

**National Geographic Learning**
20 Channel Center St.
Boston, MA 02210
USA

Cengage Learning is a leading provider of customized learning solutions with office locations around the globe, including Andover, Melbourne, Mexico City, Stamford (CT), Toronto, Hong Kong, New Delhi, Seoul, Singapore, and Tokyo. Locate your local office at **www.cengage.com/global**

Cengage Learning products are represented in Canada by Nelson Education, Ltd.

Visit National Geographic Learning online at **ngl.cengage.com**
For product information, visit our website at **www.cengageasia.com**

Printed in Singapore
2 3 4 5 6 7 8 17 16 15 14

*The author and publisher would like to thank the following reviewers:*

**UNITED STATES** Adrianne Aiko Thompson, Miami Dade College, Miami, Florida; **Gokhan Alkanat**, Auburn University at Montgomery, Alabama; **Nikki Ashcraft**, Shenandoah University, VA; **Karin Avila-John**, University of Dayton, Ohio; **Shirley Baker**, Alliant International University, California; **John Baker**, Oakland Community College, Michigan; **Evina Baquiran Torres**, Zoni Language Centers, New York; **Michelle Bell**, University of South Florida, Florida; **Nancy Boyer**, Golden West College, California; **Carol Brutza**, Gateway Community College, Connecticut; **Sarah Camp**, University of Kentucky, Center for ESL, Kentucky; **Maria Caratini**, Eastfield College, Texas; **Ana Maria Cepero**, Miami Dade College, Florida; **Daniel Chaboya**, Tulsa Community College, Oklahoma; **Patricia Chukwueke**, English Language Institute – UCSD Extension, California; **Julia A. Correia**, Henderson State University, Connecticut; **Suzanne Crisci**, Bunker Hill Community College, Massachusetts; **Katie Crowder**, University of North Texas, Texas; **Lynda Dalgish**, Concordia College, New York; **Jeffrey Diluglio**, Center for English Language and Orientation Programs: Boston University, Massachusetts; **Tim DiMatteo**, Southern New Hampshire University, New Hampshire; **Scott Dirks**, Kaplan International Center at Harvard Square, Massachusetts; **Margo Downey**, Center for English Language and Orientation Programs: Boston University, Massachusetts; **John Drezek**, Richland College, Texas; **Anwar El-Issa**, Antelope Valley College, California; **Anrisa Fannin**, The International Education Center at Diablo Valley College, California; **Jennie Farnell**, University of Connecticut, American Language Program, Connecticut; **Mark Fisher**, Lone Star College, Texas; **Celeste Flowers**, University of Central Arkansas, Arkansas; **John Fox**, English Language Institute, Georgia; **Pradel R. Frank**, Miami Dade College, Florida; **Sally Gearheart**, Santa Rosa Jr. College, California; **Karen Grubbs**, ELS Language Centers, Florida; **Joni Hagigeorges**, Salem State University, Massachusetts; **Valerie Heming**, University of Central Missouri, Missouri; **Mary Hill**, North Shore Community College, Massachusetts; **Harry L. Holden**, North Lake College, Texas; **Ingrid Holm**, University of Massachusetts Amherst, Massachusetts; **Marianne Hsu Santelli**, Middlesex County College, New Jersey; **Katie Hurter**, Lone Star College – North Harris, Texas; **Justin Jernigan**, Georgia Gwinnett College, Georgia; **Barbara A. Jonckheere**, American Language Institute at California State University, Long Beach, California; **Susan Jordan**, Fisher College, Massachusetts; **Maria Kasparova**, Bergen Community College, New Jersey; **Gail Kellersberger**, University of Houston-Downtown, Texas; **Christina Kelso**, Austin Peay State University, Tennessee; **Daryl Kinney**, Los Angeles City College, California; **Leslie Kosel Eckstein**, Hillsborough Community College, Florida; **Beth Kozbial Ernst**, University of Wisconsin-Eau Claire, Wisconsin; **Jennifer Lacroix**, Center for English Language and Orientation Programs: Boston University, Massachusetts; **Stuart Landers**, Missouri State University, Missouri; **Margaret V. Layton**, University of Nevada, Reno Intensive English Language Center, Nevada; **Heidi Lieb**, Bergen Community College, New Jersey; **Kerry Linder**, Language Studies International New York, New York; **Jenifer Lucas-Uygun**, Passaic County Community College, New Jersey; **Alison MacAdams**, Approach International Student Center, Massachusetts; **Craig Machado**, Norwalk Community College, Connecticut; **Andrew J. MacNeill**, Southwestern College, California; **Melanie A. Majeski**, Naugatuck Valley Community College, Connecticut; **Wendy Maloney**, College of DuPage, Illinois; **Chris Mares**, University of Maine – Intensive English Institute, Maine; **Josefina Mark**, Union County College, New Jersey; **Connie Mathews**, Nashville State Community College, Tennessee; **Bette Matthews**, Mid-Pacific Institute, Hawaii; **Marla McDaniels Heath**, Norwalk Community College, Connecticut; **Kimberly McGrath Moreira**, University of Miami, Florida; **Sara McKinnon**, College of Marin, California; **Christine Mekkaoui**, Pittsburg State University, Kansas; **Holly A. Milkowart**, Johnson County Community College, Kansas; **Warren Mosher**, University of Miami, Florida; **Lukas Murphy**, Westchester Community College, New York; **Elena Nehrebecki**, Hudson Community College, New Jersey; **Bjarne Nielsen**, Central Piedmont Community College, North Carolina; **David Nippoldt**, Reedley College, California; **Lucia Parsley**, Virginia Commonwealth University, Virginia; **Wendy Patriquin**, Parkland College, Illinois; **Marion Piccolomini**, Communicate With Ease, LTD, Pennsylvania; **Carolyn Prager**, Spanish-American Institute, New York; **Eileen Prince**, Prince Language Associates Incorporated, Massachusetts; **Sema Pulak**, Texas A & M University, Texas; **James T. Raby**, Clark University, Massachusetts; **Anouchka Rachelson**, Miami-Dade College, Florida; **Lynn Ramage Schaefer**, University of Central Arkansas, Arkansas; **Sherry Rasmussen**, DePaul University, Illinois; **Amy Renehan**, University of Washington, Washington; **Esther Robbins**, Prince George's Community College, Pennsylvania; **Helen Roland**, Miami Dade College, Florida; **Linda Roth**, Vanderbilt University English Language Center, Tennessee; **Janine Rudnick**, El Paso Community College, Texas; **Rita Rutkowski Weber**, University of Wisconsin – Milwaukee, Wisconsin; **Elena Sapp**, INTO Oregon State University, Oregon; **Margaret Shippey**, Miami Dade College, Florida; **Lisa Sieg**, Murray State University, Kentucky; **Alison Stamps**, ESL Center at Mississippi State University, Mississippi; **Peggy Street**, ELS Language Centers, Miami, Florida; **Lydia Streiter**, York College Adult Learning Center, New York; **Nicholas Taggart**, Arkansas State University, Arkansas; **Marcia Takacs**, Coastline Community College, California; **Tamara Teffeteller**, University of California Los Angeles, American Language Center, California; **Rebecca Toner**, English Language Programs, University of Pennsylvania, Pennsylvania; **William G. Trudeau**, Missouri Southern State University, Missouri; **Troy Tucker**, Edison State College, Florida; **Maria Vargas-O'Neel**, Miami Dade College, Florida; **Amerca Vazquez**, Miami Dade College, Florida; **Alison Vinande**, Modesto Junior College, California; **Christie Ward**, Intensive English Language Program, Central Connecticut State University, Connecticut; **Colin S. Ward**, Lone Star College-North Harris, Texas; **Denise L. Warner**, Lansing Community College, Michigan; **Wendy Wish-Bogue**, Valencia Community College, Florida; **Cissy Wong**, Sacramento City College, California; **Kimberly Yoder**, Kent State University, ESL Center, Ohio.

**ASIA** Teoh Swee Ai, Universiti Teknologi Mara, Malaysia; **Nor Azni Abdullah**, Universiti Teknologi Mara, Malaysia; **Thomas E. Bieri**, Nagoya College, Japan; **Paul Bournhonesque**, Seoul National University of Technology, Korea; **Michael C. Cheng**, National Chengchi University; **Fu-Dong Chiou**, National Taiwan University; **Derek Currie**, Korea University, Sejong Institute of Foreign Language Studies, Korea; **Christoph A. Hafner**, City University of Hong Kong, Hong Kong; **Wenhua Hsu**, I-Shou University; **Helen Huntley**, Hanoi University, Vietnam; **Rob Higgens**, Ritsumeikan University, Japan; **Shih Fan Kao**, JinWen University of Science and Technology; **Ikuko Kashiwabara**, Osaka Electro-Communication University, Japan; **Richard S. Lavin**, Prefectural University of Kumamoto, Japan; **Mike Lay**, American Institute, Cambodia; **Byoung-Kyo Lee**, Yonsei University, Korea; **Lin Li**, Capital Normal University, China; **Hudson Murrell**, Baiko Gakuin University, Japan; **Keiichi Narita**, Niigata University, Japan; **Huynh Thi Ai Nguyen**, Vietnam USA Society, Vietnam; **James Pham**, IDP Phnom Penh, Cambodia; **Duncan Rose**, British Council, Singapore; **Simone Samuels**, The Indonesia Australia Language Foundation Jakarta, Indonesia; **Wang Songmei**, Beijing Institute of Education Faculty, China; **Chien-Wen Jenny Tseng**, National Sun Yat-Sen University; **Hajime Uematsu**, Hirosaki University, Japan

**AUSTRALIA** Susan Austin, University of South Australia, **Joanne Cummins**, Swinburne College; **Pamela Humphreys**, Griffith University

**LATIN AMERICA AND THE CARIBBEAN** Ramon Aguilar, Universidad Tecnológica de Hermosillo, México; **Livia de Araujo Donnini Rodrigues**, University of São Paolo, Brazil; **Cecilia Avila**, Universidad de Xapala, México; Beth Bartlett, Centro Cultural Colombo Americano, Cali, Colombia; **Raúl Billini**, Colegio Loyola, Dominican Republic; **Nohora Edith Bryan**, Universidad de La Sabana, Colombia; **Raquel Hernández Cantú**, Instituto Tecnológico de Monterrey, Mexico; **Millie Commander**, Inter American University of Puerto Rico, Puerto Rico; **Edwin Marín-Arroyo**, Instituto Tecnológico de Costa Rica; **Rosario Mena**, Instituto Cultural Dominico-Americano, Dominican Republic; **Elizabeth Ortiz Lozada**, COPEI-COPOL English Institute, Ecuador; **Gilberto Rios Zamora**, Sinaloa State Language Center, Mexico; **Patricia Veciños**, El Instituto Cultural Argentino Norteamericano, Argentina

**MIDDLE EAST AND NORTH AFRICA** Tom Farkas, American University of Cairo, Egypt; **Ghada Hozayen**, Arab Academy for Science, Technology and Maritime Transport, Egypt

# Scope and Sequence

| Grammar | Speaking Skills | Viewing | Critical Thinking Skills |
|---|---|---|---|
| Verb + Gerund<br><br>Verb + Object + Infinitive | Using Fillers<br><br>Expressing a Lack of Knowledge<br><br>**Student to Student:**<br>Congratulating the Group<br><br>**Presentation Skills:**<br>Varying Your Voice Volume | **Video:**<br>*Farm Restoration*<br><br>Viewing for Main Ideas<br><br>Viewing for Specific Information<br><br>Note-Taking | Understanding and Using Buzzwords in a Conversation<br><br>Interviewing Classmates and Analyzing Feedback<br><br>Relating Unit Content to Personal Opinions<br><br>Comparing and Contrasting Cultures Using Unit Content<br><br>Analyzing and Discussing Web Sites<br><br>**Critical Thinking Focus:**<br>Evaluating Numbers and Statistics |
| Using Connectors to Add and Emphasize Information<br><br>Using Connectors of Concession | Showing that You are Following a Conversation<br><br>Digressing from the Topic<br><br>**Student to Student:**<br>Asking Sensitive Questions<br><br>**Presentation Skills:**<br>Dealing with Difficult Questions | **Video:**<br>*The Black Diamonds of Provence*<br><br>Viewing for Main Ideas<br><br>Note-Taking While Viewing | Orally Summarizing Information from Notes<br><br>Relating Unit Content to Personal Experiences<br><br>Applying New Grammar to Discussions about Finance<br><br>Understanding and Analyzing Visuals<br><br>Interpreting Information about Budgets<br><br>**Critical Thinking Focus:**<br>Summarizing |
| Phrasal Verbs<br><br>Three-Word Phrasal Verbs | Expressing Uncertainty<br><br>Showing Understanding<br><br>Sharing Advice<br><br>**Student to Student:**<br>Going First<br><br>**Presentation Skills:**<br>Relating to Your Audience | **Video:**<br>*Paraguay Shaman*<br><br>Applying Prior Knowledge to Video Content<br><br>Viewing for Main Ideas<br><br>Viewing for Specific Details | Proposing Solutions for Health Problems<br><br>Relating Unit Content to Personal Experiences<br><br>Evaluating a Health-Related Lawsuit<br><br>Using New Grammar and Vocabulary while Role-Playing a Scenario<br><br>Expressing and Explaining Opinions<br><br>**Critical Thinking Focus:**<br>Asking Questions for Further Research |
| Subject-Verb Agreement with Quantifiers<br><br>Present Participle Phrases | Enumerating<br><br>Checking Background Knowledge<br><br>**Student to Student:**<br>Joining a Group<br><br>**Presentation Skills:**<br>Using Gestures | **Video:**<br>*Animal Minds*<br><br>Viewing for Main Ideas<br><br>Viewing for Specific Information<br><br>Sequencing Events | Making Comparisons about Human and Animal Intelligence<br><br>Practicing Memory-Building Techniques<br><br>Making Inferences<br><br>Organizing Ideas for a Presentation<br><br>Using New Grammar to Summarize Unit Content<br><br>**Critical Thinking Focus:**<br>Questioning Results |
| Causative Verbs<br><br>Subjunctive Verbs with *That* Clauses | Confirming Understanding<br><br>Giving Recommendations<br><br>**Student to Student:**<br>Expressing Opinions<br><br>**Presentation Skills:**<br>Preparing Visuals for Display | **Video:**<br>*Slow Food*<br><br>Viewing for Main Ideas<br><br>Viewing to Complete Direct Quotations | Proposing Solutions for Food Shortages<br><br>Expressing Opinions about Unit Content<br><br>Deducing Meaning from Context<br><br>Understanding Visuals<br><br>Creating Effective Visuals<br><br>**Critical Thinking Focus:**<br>Remaining Objective |

Each unit consists of two lessons which include the following sections:

Building Vocabulary
Using Vocabulary
Developing Listening Skills
Exploring Spoken English
Speaking (called "Engage" in Lesson B)

An **academic pathway** is clearly labeled for learners, starting with formal listening (e.g., lectures) and moving to a more informal context (e.g., a conversation between students in a study group).

The **"Exploring the Theme"** section provides a visual introduction to the unit and encourages learners to think critically and share ideas about the unit topic.

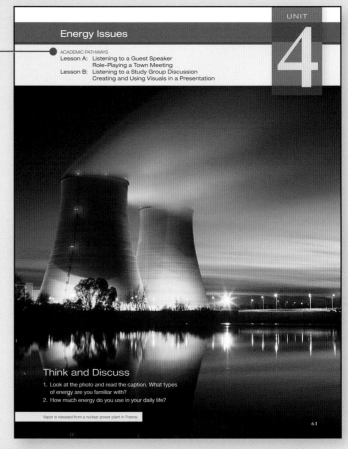

UNIT 4

Energy Issues

ACADEMIC PATHWAYS
Lesson A:  Listening to a Guest Speaker
           Role-Playing a Town Meeting
Lesson B:  Listening to a Study Group Discussion
           Creating and Using Visuals in a Presentation

**Think and Discuss**

1. Look at the photo and read the caption. What types of energy are you familiar with?
2. How much energy do you use in your daily life?

Vapor is released from a nuclear power plant in France.

61

**Exploring the Theme:**
**Energy Issues**

A | Look at the photos and read the captions. Then answer the questions.

1. How do you think energy use has changed over time?
2. In the future, do you think you will be using more or less electricity than you do now? Why do you think so?
3. Would you be willing to live next to a large energy facility such as a nuclear power plant or wind farm? Explain your answer.

**Big Power, Big Risks**

By the year 2030, the demand for energy is expected to be double what it was in the year 2000. Providing the enormous quantity of energy the world needs is a difficult task, and there is often risk for workers, the public, and the environment.

In this village, lights shine from nearly every house. However, the world is still far away from providing inexpensive electricity. In fact, about one in four people still have no electricity at all.

Wind power provides energy to farms and homes in Abilene, Texas.

62 | UNIT 4

ENERGY ISSUES | 63

**Key academic and high-frequency vocabulary** is introduced, practiced, and expanded throughout each unit. Lessons A and B each present and practice 10 terms.

A **"Developing Listening Skills"** section follows a before, during, and after listening approach to give learners the tools necessary to master listening skills for a variety of contexts.

**Listening activities** encourage learners to listen for and consolidate key information, reinforcing the language, and allowing learners to think critically about the information they hear.

---

**LESSON A   BUILDING VOCABULARY**

🎧 track 2-2   **A | Meaning from Context.** Read and listen to the news report about the Deepwater Horizon oil spill. Notice the words in blue. These are words you will hear and use in Lesson A.

On April 20, 2010, one of the worst oil spills in history began in the Gulf of Mexico. The spill occurred at an oil rig, called the Deepwater Horizon, which is owned by the BP company. A buildup of pressure caused natural gas to shoot up suddenly from the ocean floor. The gas **triggered** a terrible explosion and a fire on the oil rig. After the explosion, the crew **abandoned** the platform and escaped in lifeboats. Unfortunately, eleven workers were never found.

*A beach in the United States is covered with oil after the Deepwater Horizon oil spill.*

For weeks, no one was sure just how much oil was being **released** into the Gulf of Mexico. Gradually, information about the damage from the oil spill **emerged**. It was discovered that between 50,000 to 60,000 barrels of oil a day were flowing into the Gulf. **Experts** from BP and other organizations tried to stop the spill, but it continued for nearly three months. By the time the leak was stopped, the beautiful blue waters of the Gulf had been **contaminated** with nearly 5 million barrels of oil.

The disaster did serious harm to the fishing and tourism industries in the southern United States. Pictures of birds that had been **exposed** to the thick oil appeared daily in the news. The American public **reacted** angrily, and the spill created a huge **controversy**. Some people even wanted to stop oil companies from drilling in the Gulf of Mexico. BP set aside 20 billion dollars to **compensate** fishermen, hotel owners, and store owners whose businesses were impacted by the spill.

**B |** Match each word in blue from exercise **A** with its definition. Use your dictionary to help you.

1. triggered (v.) _____
2. abandoned (v.) _____
3. released (v.) _____
4. emerged (v.) _____
5. experts (n.) _____
6. contaminated (v.) _____
7. exposed (v.) _____
8. reacted (v.) _____
9. controversy (n.) _____
10. compensate (v.) _____

a. to pay someone to replace lost money or things
b. became known; appeared
c. responded to
d. caused an event to begin to happen
e. left a place, thing, or person permanently
f. people who are very skilled or who know a lot about a particular subject
g. entered the surrounding atmosphere or area; freed
h. a disagreement, especially about a public policy or moral issue that people feel strongly about
i. made something dirty, harmful, or dangerous because of chemicals or radiation
j. placed in a dangerous situation

64 | UNIT 4

---

**LESSON A   DEVELOPING LISTENING SKILLS**

### Before Listening

👥 **Predicting Content.** Work with a partner. Look at the map and diagram. Discuss the questions.

1. Use your dictionary and look up these terms: *containment, radiation, radioactive, half-life.* How do you predict these words will be used in the lecture?
2. Locate the containment structure in the diagram. Why do you think this structure is important? Explain your ideas.

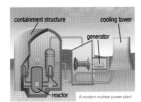

BELARUS   RUSSIA
CHERNOBYL NUCLEAR POWER PLANT
UKRAINE

containment structure   cooling tower
generator
reactor
*A modern nuclear power plant*

### Listening: A Guest Speaker

**Critical Thinking Focus: Using an Outline to Take Notes**

Using an outline can help you take organized and clear notes. In an outline, indicate main ideas with Roman numerals (I, II, III) and capital letters (A, B, C). Indicate details with numbers. As information becomes more specific, move it to the right.

🎧 track 2-3   **A |** Listen to the introduction to a lecture about the Chernobyl nuclear disaster. Read the outline as you listen.

I. Background
   A. 1970s & 1980s: Soviet Union developed nuclear technology
   B. 1986: 25 plants w/ safety probs.
II. Chernobyl disaster
   A. Causes
      1. Mistakes during safety test
      2. No containment building to limit fire and radiation
   B. Result: explosion→people dead

👥 **B | Discussion.** With a partner, discuss the questions. Refer to the outline in exercise **A**.

1. What topics did the introduction cover?
2. Which items are main ideas? Which items are details?

🎧 track 2-4   **C | Listening for Main Ideas.** Listen to the entire lecture and answer the questions.

1. Check (✔) each effect of the explosion that the speaker mentions.
   _____ a. People were forced to leave their homes.
   _____ b. Animals died from exposure to radiation.
   _____ c. Young people became ill with thyroid cancer.
   _____ d. Billions of dollars were spent on health and cleanup costs.
   _____ e. Modern nuclear power plants are built with containment structures.
2. What happened to the town of Pripyat?
   a. It was abandoned.
   b. It burned to the ground.
   c. It was turned into a tourist attraction.
3. What is surprising about Chernobyl today?
   a. The residents of Pripyat have returned.
   b. Many animals have come back to the area.
   c. The radiation from the explosion has disappeared.

🎧 track 2-4   **D | Outlining.** Listen again. Continue the outline from exercise **A** on page 66. Complete the outline with details from the lecture. (*See page 206 of the Independent Student Handbook for more information on outlining.*)

C. The Chernobyl plant today
   1. Still extremely _____
   2. There are plans to build a _____
D. Radioactivity
   1. Many areas still contaminated with cesium _____
   2. Half-life of _____ years
E. The exclusion zone today
   1. _____ people live there
   2. Animals have returned, for ex. _____

### After Listening

👥 **Discussion.** With a partner, answer the questions. Use your notes as well as your own ideas.

1. Describe the town of Pripyat before and after the disaster.
2. These days, a small number of tourists travel to Chernobyl. Would you go there if you had the opportunity?

**LESSON A** | EXPLORING SPOKEN ENGLISH

## Language Function

**Emphasizing Important Information**

Here are some expressions used to emphasize important information.

| | |
|---|---|
| Don't forget that . . . | I would like to point out that . . . |
| Let me stress that . . . | You need to remember that . . . |
| I want to emphasize that . . . | It is important to note/remember that . . . |
| I would like to stress that . . . | |

**A** | In the lecture about Chernobyl, the speaker used a number of useful expressions to emphasize her point. Listen to the excerpts and fill in the missing expressions.

1. _____ Chernobyl had no containment structure. This building would have limited the fire and contained the radioactivity.
2. Thyroid cancer can be cured, but _____ survivors must spend a lifetime taking medication.
3. _____, however, that it will be decades before large numbers of people are allowed to come back and live in the exclusion zone.

Wild horses, called Przewalski horses, walk through the Chernobyl exclusion zone. These horses are extinct in the wild and can only be found in a few nature reserves and in the Chernobyl exclusion zone.

**B** | Form a group with two other students. Choose one of the types of energy below and read the facts. Then tell the members of your group what you know about your energy source. Add your own ideas. Emphasize the fact that you think is the most interesting.

> Oil prices are rising. For example, it cost me almost $60 to put gas in my car yesterday. Last year, it would have cost me only $40. Still, it is important to remember that . . .

**Oil**
- The price of oil is rising.
- Oil spills pollute the environment.
- The top three oil-producing countries in the world are Saudi Arabia, Russia, and the United States.

**Coal**
- Coal deposits in the United States contain more energy than all the world's oil reserves combined.
- Coal is a relatively inexpensive energy source.
- Coal mining is dangerous. Between 1969 and 2000, more than 20,000 coal miners were killed.

**Wind**
- Wind power is clean, but is sometimes very noisy.
- The world will never run out of wind.
- Denmark gets 20 percent of its electricity from wind power.

68 | UNIT 4

ENERGY ISSUES | 69

The **"Exploring Spoken English"** section allows students to examine and practice specific grammar points and language functions from the unit while enabling them to sharpen their listening and speaking skills.

Lesson A closes with a **full page of "Speaking" activities** including pair and group work activities, increasing learner confidence when communicating in English.

**A variety of activity types** simulate the academic classroom, where multiple skills must be applied simultaneously for success.

## SPEAKING

### Role-Playing a Town Meeting

**A** | Form a group with three other students. You will role-play a city council meeting about building a nuclear power plant. Read the situation and the role cards. Assign two students to each role.

**Situation:** The city council has approved a plan to build a nuclear power plant in your city. A small group of residents are against the plan. They are going to meet with city council members to discuss their concerns.

**Role #1: Residents against the Nuclear Power Plant**

1. Nuclear power plants aren't safe. We don't want a nuclear accident to happen here.
2. Nuclear power plants produce waste that is dangerous for many years.
3. People who live near a nuclear power plant might get cancer.

**Role #2: City Council Members**

1. Nuclear safety technology has greatly advanced in recent years.
2. France, Belgium, and Slovakia rely on nuclear power for more than 50 percent of their electricity. There have been no big nuclear accidents in those countries.
3. Nuclear power could help us stop using oil.

**B** | Work with the group member who shares your role. Think of more arguments to support your point. In addition, try to think of responses to the other side's arguments.

> I think they will say that . . . .

> If they say that, we should emphasize that . . .

**C** | Role-Playing. Role-play the discussion in your group. Use expressions of emphasis when appropriate.

> Thank you for meeting with us. We have a few concerns about this nuclear power plant.

> I understand. First of all, let me stress that we will do everything possible to make this power plant safe.

**Student to Student: Conceding a Point**

In a debate or discussion, people often argue from different points of view. If an argument is very convincing to you, you can let the other person know that you agree with their point or that you accept that their point is true. Here are some expressions to concede a point.

*Good point.*
*Fair enough.*
*I'll give you that.*

ENERGY ISSUES | 71

● The **"Viewing" section** works as a content-bridge between Lesson A and Lesson B and includes two pages of activities based on a fascinating video from National Geographic.

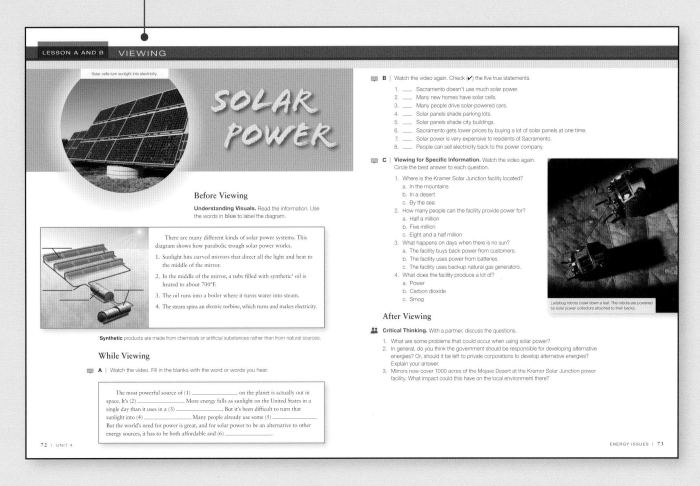

LESSON A AND B  VIEWING

Solar cells turn sunlight into electricity.

# SOLAR POWER

### Before Viewing

**Understanding Visuals.** Read the information. Use the words in blue to label the diagram.

There are many different kinds of solar power systems. This diagram shows how parabolic trough solar power works.

1. Sunlight hits curved mirrors that direct all the light and heat to the middle of the mirror.
2. In the middle of the mirror, a tube filled with synthetic[1] oil is heated to about 700°F.
3. The oil runs into a boiler where it turns water into steam.
4. The steam spins an electric turbine, which turns and makes electricity.

¹**Synthetic** products are made from chemicals or artificial substances rather than from natural sources.

### While Viewing

**A** | Watch the video. Fill in the blanks with the word or words you hear.

The most powerful source of (1) _____ on the planet is actually out in space. It's (2) _____. More energy falls as sunlight on the United States in a single day than it uses in a (3) _____. But it's been difficult to turn that sunlight into (4) _____. Many people already use some (5) _____. But the world's need for power is great, and for solar power to be an alternative to other energy sources, it has to be both affordable and (6) _____.

**B** | Watch the video again. Check (✔) the five true statements.

1. ____ Sacramento doesn't use much solar power.
2. ____ Many new homes have solar cells.
3. ____ Many people drive solar-powered cars.
4. ____ Solar panels shade parking lots.
5. ____ Solar panels shade city buildings.
6. ____ Sacramento gets lower prices by buying a lot of solar panels at one time.
7. ____ Solar power is very expensive to residents of Sacramento.
8. ____ People can sell electricity back to the power company.

**C** | **Viewing for Specific Information.** Watch the video again. Circle the best answer to each question.

1. Where is the Kramer Solar Junction facility located?
   a. In the mountains
   b. In a desert
   c. By the sea
2. How many people can the facility provide power for?
   a. Half a million
   b. Five million
   c. Eight and a half million
3. What happens on days when there is no sun?
   a. The facility buys back power from customers.
   b. The facility uses power from batteries.
   c. The facility uses backup natural gas generators.
4. What does the facility produce a lot of?
   a. Power
   b. Carbon dioxide
   c. Smog

Ladybug robots crawl down a leaf. The robots are powered by solar power collectors attached to their backs.

### After Viewing

**Critical Thinking.** With a partner, discuss the questions.

1. What are some problems that could occur when using solar power?
2. In general, do you think the government should be responsible for developing alternative energies? Or, should it be left to private corporations to develop alternative energies? Explain your answer.
3. Mirrors now cover 1000 acres of the Mojave Desert at the Kramer Solar Junction power facility. What impact could this have on the local environment there?

72 | UNIT 4

ENERGY ISSUES | 73

● **A DVD for each level** contains 10 authentic videos from National Geographic specially adapted for English language learners.

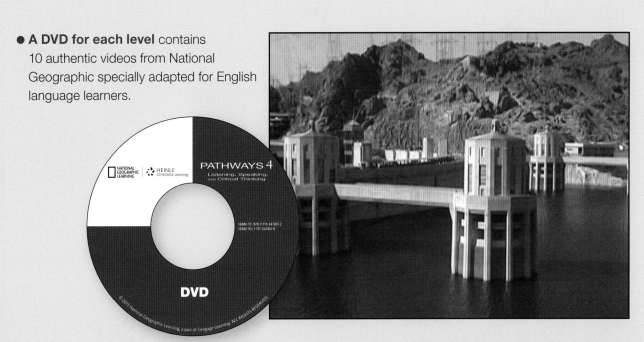

NATIONAL GEOGRAPHIC LEARNING | HEINLE CENGAGE Learning

PATHWAYS 4
Listening, Speaking, and Critical Thinking

ISBN-13: 978-1-111-34780-2
ISBN-10: 1-111-34780-8

DVD

© 2013 National Geographic Learning, a part of Cengage Learning. ALL RIGHTS RESERVED.

**Critical thinking activities** are integrated in every unit, encouraging continuous engagement in developing academic skills.

An **"Engage" section** at the end of the unit challenges learners with an end-of-unit presentation project. Speaking tips are offered for formal and informal group communication, instructing students to interact appropriately in different academic situations.

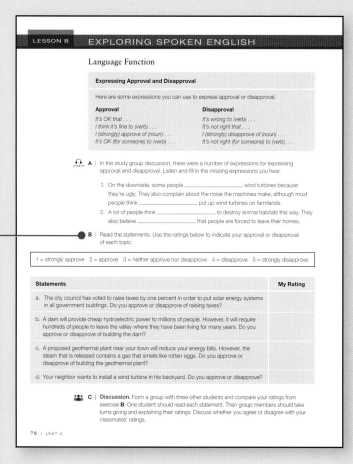

LESSON B  |  EXPLORING SPOKEN ENGLISH

### Language Function

**Expressing Approval and Disapproval**

Here are some expressions you can use to express approval or disapproval.

| Approval | Disapproval |
|---|---|
| It's OK that . . . | It's wrong to (verb) . . . |
| I think it's fine to (verb) . . . | It's not right that . . . |
| I (strongly) approve of (noun) . . . | I (strongly) disapprove of (noun) . . . |
| It's OK (for someone) to (verb) . . . | It's not right (for someone) to (verb) . . . |

🎧 Unit 2-11  **A** | In the study group discussion, there were a number of expressions for expressing approval and disapproval. Listen and fill in the missing expressions you hear.

1. On the downside, some people _____ wind turbines because they're ugly. They also complain about the noise the machines make, although most people think _____ put up wind turbines on farmlands.

2. A lot of people think _____ to destroy animal habitats this way. They also believe _____ that people are forced to leave their homes.

**B** | Read the statements. Use the ratings below to indicate your approval or disapproval of each topic.

1 = strongly approve   2 = approve   3 = neither approve nor disapprove   4 = disapprove   5 = strongly disapprove

| Statements | My Rating |
|---|---|
| a. The city council has voted to raise taxes by one percent in order to put solar energy systems in all government buildings. Do you approve or disapprove of raising taxes? | |
| b. A dam will provide cheap hydroelectric power to millions of people. However, it will require hundreds of people to leave the valley where they have been living for many years. Do you approve or disapprove of building the dam? | |
| c. A proposed geothermal plant near your town will reduce your energy bills. However, the steam that is released contains a gas that smells like rotten eggs. Do you approve or disapprove of building the geothermal plant? | |
| d. Your neighbor wants to install a wind turbine in his backyard. Do you approve or disapprove? | |

**C** | **Discussion.** Form a group with three other students and compare your ratings from exercise **B**. One student should read each statement. Then group members should take turns giving and explaining their ratings. Discuss whether you agree or disagree with your classmates' ratings.

78 | UNIT 4

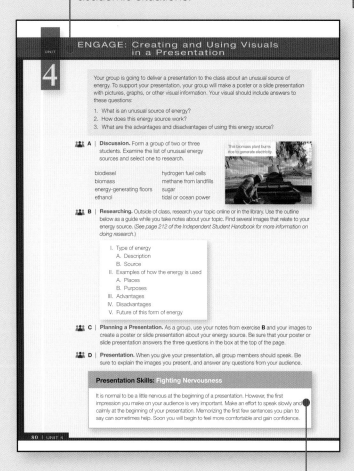

UNIT 4

ENGAGE: Creating and Using Visuals in a Presentation

Your group is going to deliver a presentation to the class about an unusual source of energy. To support your presentation, your group will make a poster or a slide presentation with pictures, graphs, or other visual information. Your visual should include answers to these questions:

1. What is an unusual source of energy?
2. How does this energy source work?
3. What are the advantages and disadvantages of using this energy source?

**A** | **Discussion.** Form a group of two or three students. Examine the list of unusual energy sources and select one to research.

biodiesel   hydrogen fuel cells
biomass   methane from landfills
energy-generating floors   sugar
ethanol   tidal or ocean power

This biomass plant burns rice to generate electricity.

**B** | **Researching.** Outside of class, research your topic online or in the library. Use the outline below as a guide while you take notes about your topic. Find several images that relate to your energy source. (See page 212 of the Independent Student Handbook for more information on doing research.)

I. Type of energy
   A. Description
   B. Source
II. Examples of how the energy is used
   A. Places
   B. Purposes
III. Advantages
IV. Disadvantages
V. Future of this form of energy

**C** | **Planning a Presentation.** As a group, use your notes from exercise **B** and your images to create a poster or slide presentation about your energy source. Be sure that your poster or slide presentation answers the three questions in the box at the top of the page.

**D** | **Presentation.** When you give your presentation, all group members should speak. Be sure to explain the images you present, and answer any questions from your audience.

**Presentation Skills: Fighting Nervousness**

It is normal to be a little nervous at the beginning of a presentation. However, the first impression you make on your audience is very important. Make an effort to speak slowly and calmly at the beginning of your presentation. Memorizing the first few sentences you plan to say can sometimes help. Soon you will begin to feel more comfortable and gain confidence.

80 | UNIT 4

**"Presentation Skills" boxes** offer helpful tips and suggestions for successful academic presentations.

A 19-page **"Independent Student Handbook"** is conveniently located in the back of the book and provides helpful self-study strategies for students to become better independent learners.

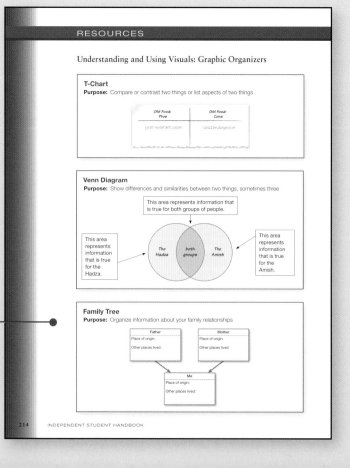

RESOURCES

### Understanding and Using Visuals: Graphic Organizers

**T-Chart**
**Purpose:** Compare or contrast two things or list aspects of two things

| GM Food: Pros | GM Food: Cons |
|---|---|
| pest-resistant crops | could be dangerous |

**Venn Diagram**
**Purpose:** Show differences and similarities between two things, sometimes three

This area represents information that is true for both groups of people.

This area represents information that is true for the Hadza.

The Hadza | both groups | The Amish

This area represents information that is true for the Amish.

**Family Tree**
**Purpose:** Organize information about your family relationships

Father — Place of origin: / Other places lived:
Mother — Place of origin: / Other places lived:
Me — Place of origin: / Other places lived:

214   INDEPENDENT STUDENT HANDBOOK

## For the Teacher:

Perfect for integrating language practice with exciting visuals, **video clips from National Geographic** bring the sights and sounds of our world into the classroom.

**The Assessment CD-ROM with Exam*View*®** is a test-generating software program with a data bank of ready-made questions designed to allow teachers to assess students quickly and effectively.

Bringing a new dimension to the language learning classroom, the **Classroom Presentation Tool CD-ROM** makes instruction clearer and learning easier through interactive activities, audio and video clips, and Presentation Worksheets.

A **Teacher's Guide** is available in an easy-to-use format and includes teacher's notes, expansion activities, and answer keys for activities in the student book.

## For the Student:

The **Student Book** helps students achieve academic success in and outside of the classroom.

**Audio CDs** contain the audio recordings for the exercises in the student books.

Powered by MyELT, the **Online Workbook** has both teacher-led and self-study options. It contains 10 National Geographic video clips, supported by interactive, automatically graded activities that practice the skills learned in the student books.

Visit elt.heinle.com/pathways for additional teacher and student resources.

# CREDITS

## LISTENING AND TEXT

**104:** Adapted from "The Hadza," by Michael Finkel: National Geographic Magazine, December 2009, **106-107, 111:** Adapted from "Bhutan's Enlightened Experiment" by Brook Larmer: National Geographic Magazine, March 2008, **110:** Adapted from "Spread of the Amish" by National Geographic Staff: National Geographic Blog Central, July 8, 2009, **114:** Adapted from "Disappearing Languages: Enduring Voices Project," National Geographic Web site, January 2011, **115-117:** Adapted from "Native Lands," by Charles Bowden: National Geographic Magazine, August 2010,

**118:** Adapted from "'Spectacular' Three-Cat Monolith Unearthed in Mexico," by Ker Than: National Geographic Daily News, August 1, 2011, **118:** Adapted from "Machu Picchu's Mysteries Continue to Lure Explorers," by Kelly Hearn and Jason Golomb: National Geographic Web site, **124, 126-127:** Adapted from "Living it Up, Paying it Down," by Mary McPeak: National Geographic Magazine, February 2005, **144, 146-147** Adapted from "The Pollution Within," by David Ewing Duncan: National Geographic Magazine, October 2006, **156-157:** Adapted from "Yosemite Climbing," by Mark Jenkins: National Geographic Magazine, May 2011, **165-167:** Adapted from "Minds of Their Own," by Virginia Morrell: National

Geographic Magazine, March 2008; **175:** Adapted from "Young Chimp Outscores College Students in Memory Test," by Malcolm Ritter: National Geographic News, December 3, 2007, **176-177** Adapted from "Remember This" by Joshua Foer: National Geographic Magazine, November 2007, **184, 186-187, 189:** Adapted from "Food: How Altered?," by Jennifer Ackerman: National Geographic Magazine, May 2002, **184:** Adapted from "Food Ark," by Charles Siebert: National Geographic Magazine, July 2011, **194-197:** Adapted from "The Global Food Crisis: The End of Plenty," by Joel K. Bourne, Jr.: National Geographic Magazine, June 2009.

## PHOTOS

**101:** Paul Nicklen/National Geographic Image Collection, **102:** Bartosz Hadyniak/iStockphoto.com, **102:** Randy Olson/National Geographic Image Collection, **103:** Lightmediation/National Geographic Image Collection, **103:** Schoeller, Martin/National Geographic Image Collection, **103:** Steve Winter/National Geographic Image Collection, **104:** Schoeller, Martin/National Geographic Image Collection, **107:** Lynsey Addario/National Geographic Image Collection, **109:** Melinda Fawver/Shutterstock.com, **109:** Carmen Martínez Banús/Maica/, **110:** Martin Thomas Photography/Alamy, **112:** YinYang/iStockphoto.com, **113:** Bruce MacQueen/Shutterstock.com, **114:** Paul Harris/John Warburton-Lee Photography/Alamy, **115:** Dave G. Houser/Corbis, **117:** Jack Dykinga/National Geographic Image Collection, **118:** Handout/Reuters, **118:** Mircea Simu/Shutterstock.com, **121:** Tyrone Turner/National Geographic Image Collection, **122:** StockLite/Shutterstock.com, **122:** Billy Hustace/Corbis, **122-123:** Tino Soriano/National Geographic Image Collection, **124:** David Mclain/National Geographic Image Collection, **124:** David McLain/National Geographic Image Collection, **126:** Blend Images (RF)/Hill Street Studios/Jupiter Images, **129:** Fedor Kondratenko/Shutterstock.com, **132:** Catherine Hansen/Photononstop/PhotoLibrary, **132:** sutsaiy/Shutterstock.com, **133:** foodfolio/Alamy, **134:** John Gress/Reuters, **136:** Aaron Lambert/Santa Maria Times/ZUMA Press/

Newscom, **139:** Frank May/dpa/Landov, **141:** Jimmy Chin/National Geographic Image Collection, **142:** Photograph by Peter Essick, **142:** John Stanmeyer LLC/National Geographic Image Collection, **142:** Jimmy Chin/National Geographic Image Collection, **142-143:** Dawn Kish/National Geographic Image Collection, **144:** Photograph by Peter Essick, **144:** Everett Collection, **146:** Peter Essick/National Geographic Image Collection, **147:** Peter Essick/National Geographic Image Collection, **148:** Photograph by Peter Essick, **148:** Peter Essick/National Geographic Image Collection, **148:** Photograph by Peter Essick, **148:** Peter Essick/National Geographic Image Collection, **150:** Rich Legg/iStockphoto, **152:** Michael Nichols/National Geographic Image Collection, **153:** Michael Edwards/Alamy, **153:** Terry Whittaker/FLPA/PhotoLibrary, **154:** dbtravel/dbimages/Alamy, **154:** Bill Hatcher/National Geographic Image Collection, **154:** Pete McBride/National Geographic Image Collection, **156:** Jimmy Chin/National Geographic Image Collection, **159:** Denis Raev/iStockphoto.com, **161:** Rod Porteous/Robert Harding World Imagery/Corbis, **163:** Vincent J. Musi/National Geographic Image Collection, **163:** Maggie Steber, **163:** Maggie Steber/National Geographic Image Collection, **164:** Uryadnikov Sergey/Shutterstock, **165:** Cohn, Ronald H/National Geographic Image Collection, **166:** Vincent J. Musi/National Geographic Image Collection, **166:** Vincent J. Musi/National Geographic Image Collection, **169:** Natursports/Shutterstock, **169:** sjlocke/iStockphoto, **169:** Christina Richards/Shutterstock.com,

**172:** sextoacto/iStockphoto, **172:** Joe Raedle/Newsmakers/Getty Images, **173:** FLPA/Alamy, **174:** Maggie Steber/National Geographic Image Collection, **175:** AP Photo/Primate Research Institute, Kyoto/Tetsuro Matsuzawa, **176:** Maggie Steber/National Geographic Image Collection, **179:** Michael Nichols/National Geographic Image Collection, **181:** Michael S. Yamashita/National Geographic Image Collection, **182:** Lee Avison/GAP Photos/Getty Images, **182:** Jim Richardson/National Geographic Image Collection, **182-183:** Fritz Hoffmann/National Geographic Image Collection, **183:** John Stanmeyer LLC/National Geographic Image Collection, **184:** Jim Richardson/National Geographic Image Collection, **186:** Jim Richardson/National Geographic Image Collection, **187:** Jim Richardson/National Geographic Image Collection, **187:** Jim Richardson/National Geographic Image Collection, **187:** Colin Monteath/Minden Pictures, **187:** nopporn/Shutterstock.com, **188:** Jim Richardson/National Geographic Image Collection, **189:** Ferran Traite Soler/istockphoto.com, **189:** Jim Richardson/National Geographic Image Collection, **190:** Ted Aljibe/Staff/AFP/Getty Images, **192:** CuboImages srl/Alamy, **192:** Marka/Alamy, **193:** Christine Webb/Alamy, **193:** Eric Risberg/AP Photo, **194:** John Stanmeyer LLC/National Geographic Image Collection, **195:** John Stanmeyer LLC/National Geographic Image Collection, **198:** tBoyan/iStockphoto, **200:** Otokimus/Shutterstock

## MAP AND ILLUSTRATION

**102-103:** National Geographic Maps; **104:** National Geographic Maps; **106:** National Geographic Maps; **106:** Atlaspix/

Shutterstock.com; **112:** National Geographic Maps; **116:** National Geographic Maps; **132, 216:** Mapping Specialists, Ltd. Madison, WI USA; **152:** National Geographic Maps; **152:** National Geographic Maps; **154:** National Geographic Maps; **162-163:** Roger Harris /

Photo Researchers, Inc.; **175:** National Geographic Maps; **190:** National Geographic Maps; **192:** Mapping Specialists, Ltd. Madison, WI USA; **196:** Sean McNaughton, NGM Staff; **208:** Bob Kayganich/illustrationonline

# Tradition and Progress

## Think and Discuss

1. What is interesting or surprising about this photo?
2. What does the word *progress* mean to you?
3. What traditions are important to you? What would happen if these traditions disappeared?

A man in Alaska uses a laptop computer while sitting on a snowbank.

101

# Exploring the Theme:
## Tradition and Progress

Look at the photos and read the captions. Then discuss the questions.

1. Which of these photos do you find the most interesting? Explain.
2. Why would people want to keep their traditions?
3. How do you think life has changed for these people over the last 10 years?

Female weavers work in Chinceros, **Peru**. The weavers keep their traditional weaving skills alive by using them in a modern way—to earn money to support their families and their town.

Peru

A woman in Kyoto, **Japan** shops for food along with her helper, a talking robot.

A teenager learns to play a new sport—basketball—near his home in Batsumber, **Mongolia**.

**Japan**

**Mongolia**

**India**

**Tanzania**

A monk talks on a cell phone at a monastery in **India**.

The Hadza people of **Tanzania** are one of the last hunter-gatherer groups on earth. Today, their traditional way of life is changing.

🎧 track 2-21 **A** | **Meaning from Context.** Read and listen to the article. Notice the words in blue. These are words you will hear and use in Lesson A.

Long ago, people lived as hunters and gatherers. Over time people learned how to grow plants and raise domestic animals. Once this happened, there was a transition to agriculture in many societies. However, even today there are groups who reject farming and continue to hunt animals and gather their own food.

The Hadza people are a group of hunter-gatherers who live in an isolated part of northern Tanzania. They have lived in the Great Rift Valley for a period of 10,000 years. The Hadza communicate in their own special language, called Hadzane.

A Hadza hunter climbs a tree to see animals in the distance.

The Hadza are not part of the modern economic system of Tanzania. When they are hungry, they can hunt or gather what they need for free. Hadza men can make a little money by displaying their hunting skills for tourists. It is an interesting contradiction that although the Hadza have very little, they share a lot. In fact, they share everything they have with others.

Tanzania

In the Great Rift Valley, modern farming has spread in recent years, and this development has had serious consequences for the Hadza. Their homeland is now only 25 percent of the size it was in the 1950s. Hunting is now more difficult for them, as there are fewer animals than before. The Hadza people anticipate that their way of life will disappear in the near future.

**B** | Write each word in blue from exercise **A** next to its definition.

1. _____ (v.) to realize in advance that an event may happen
2. _____ (adj.) not wild; kept on farms or as pets
3. _____ (n.) the results or effects of an action
4. _____ (n.) a situation in which two opposite facts are true at the same time
5. _____ (v.) showing
6. _____ (n.) farming and the processes used to take care of crops and animals
7. _____ (adj.) far away from large cities and difficult to reach
8. _____ (n.) a length of time
9. _____ (v.) to turn down or not accept
10. _____ (n.) a change

**A** | **Discussion.** With a partner, discuss the questions.

1. In many ways, the Hadza people reject the modern world. Do you know other people or groups that reject things about the modern world? Why do they reject those things?
2. Many societies transitioned from hunting and gathering to agriculture. In what ways did people's lives probably change as a result?
3. How might people such as the Hadza, who speak their own language, communicate with the outside world?

**B** | **Using a Dictionary.** Work with your partner. Find the form and definition of each vocabulary word to complete the information below. Use your dictionary to help you.

| Vocabulary Word | Related Words | Related Definitions |
|---|---|---|
| 1. anticipate (v.) | (n.) _anticipation_ | _looking forward to something_ |
| 2. agriculture (n.) | (adj.) _____ | _____ |
| 3. consequences (n.) | (adv.) _____ | _____ |
| 4. contradiction (n.) | (v.) _____ | _____ |
|  | (adj.) _____ | _____ |
| 5. displaying (v.) | (n.) _____ | _____ |
| 6. domestic (adj.) | (adj.) _____ | _____ |
| 7. isolated (adj.) | (v.) _____ | _____ |
|  | (n.) _____ | _____ |
| 8. period (n.) | (adj.) _____ | _____ |
| 9. reject (v.) | (n.) _____ | _____ |

**C** | **Self-Reflection.** Form a group with two or three other students. Discuss the questions.

1. Do you think it is rude to **contradict** your parents, teachers, or other people who have authority? What do you say if you disagree with their ideas?
2. Have you ever experienced a **rejection** such as not getting a job you wanted? Explain what happened.
3. Have you ever done something that had **consequences** you did not expect? Explain the situation.

## Before Listening

**Predicting Content.** Look at the images and read the information about Bhutan. Then answer the questions with a partner.

1. Where is Bhutan located? Is it a large or a small country?
2. What image do you see on Bhutan's flag? What do you think it means?
3. Do you think Bhutan is a modern country?
4. Bhutan is trying to measure its *Gross National Happiness*. What do you think this phrase means?

The flag of Bhutan

**Bhutan Fast Facts**

**Population:** 708,427
**Capital:** Thimphu
**Area:** 14,824 square miles
(38,394 square kilometers)

## Listening: A Student Presentation

track 2-22 **A** | **Listening for Main Ideas.** Listen to a student's presentation about the country of Bhutan. Then choose the correct answers.

1. Why did Bhutan reject the modern world?
   a. Using technology was against the law.
   b. The government wanted to avoid negative influences.
   c. The people believed they didn't need any technology.
2. What government change is happening in Bhutan?
   a. It is moving toward democracy.
   b. It is becoming an absolute monarchy.
   c. The king is taking away many of the people's powers.
3. Sompel says that cultural preservation is a challenge for Bhutan because _____.
   a. half of the population is under the age of 30
   b. many people can't read or write
   c. Bhutan produces movies about cultural issues
4. What is Sompel's attitude about Bhutan's future?
   a. It is confusing to him.
   b. It makes him feel sad.
   c. He is hopeful.

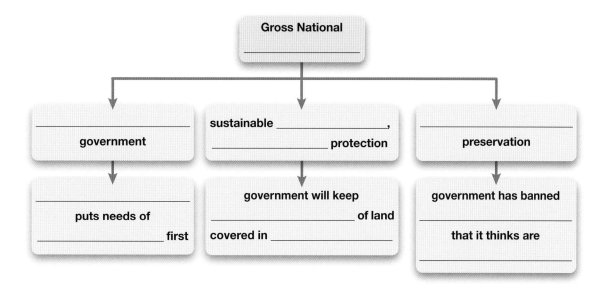

🎧 **B | Completing an Idea Map.** Listen again to part of the presentation. Complete the idea
track 2-23 map with information from the presentation. *(See page 214 of the Independent Student
Handbook for more information on using graphic organizers.)*

**Gross National**
_____

| government | sustainable _____, _____ protection | preservation |

| _____ puts needs of _____ first | government will keep _____ of land covered in _____ | government has banned _____ that it thinks are _____ |

# After Listening

👥 **Critical Thinking.** Form a group with two or three other students. Discuss the questions.

1. Do you think that the decision to open up Bhutan to the modern world was the correct
   decision? Explain.
2. Bhutanese people were allowed to watch TV for the first time in 1999. If it had been your
   decision to make, which television programs would have been shown first? Which ones
   would have been shown later or not at all? Give reasons for your decisions.
3. What does a government have to do to make sure its citizens are happy? Brainstorm some
   ideas with your group.

Children play video games in a Thimphu café.

**Student to Student:**
**Congratulating**
**the Group**

If you feel your group has
done a good job on a task,
use these expressions to
congratulate everyone.

*Nice job, everybody!*
*We make a great team!*
*Great going, gang!*
*Way to go, guys!*

## Language Function

### Using Fillers

When we speak, we sometimes forget a word or need a moment to think about what we want to say next. In these situations, we use fillers to fill the gaps in the conversation.

**Informal**

*. . . umm . . .*

*. . . oh, you know . . .*

*. . . hang on . . .*

*. . . it's on the tip of my tongue . . .*

**More Formal**

*. . . let me think . . .*

*. . . just a moment . . .*

*. . . how should I put it . . .*

*. . . oh, what's the word . . .*

**track 2-24** **A** | In the student presentation, the speaker uses a number of fillers. Listen to the sentences and fill in the missing expressions.

1. He wants our country's development to be guided by . . . _____
   . . . oh yes, *Gross National Happiness*.
2. There are four parts . . . _____ . . . four "pillars" to this approach: good government, sustainable development, environmental protection, and cultural preservation.

**B** | Work with a partner. Take turns saying the sentences from exercise **A**, using different fillers to fill the pauses.

**C** | **Self-Reflection.** With your partner, take turns answering the questions below. Use fillers to allow yourself extra time to answer.

Where did you go on your last vacation?

Oh, let me think . . . I went to Buenos Aires.

1. Where did you go on your last vacation?
2. What was your favorite TV show when you were a child?
3. What did you have for dinner last night?
4. Who was your favorite teacher?
5. Who was the last person you danced with?
6. What was the title of the last book you read?

**D** | With your partner, read the definition of *buzzword* and the four buzzwords in the box. Then practice the conversations below. When you see a blank, use a buzzword. Continue each conversation and use fillers as needed.

A **buzzword** is a word or expression that has become common in a particular field and is being used often by the media. For example:

- **the blogosphere:** all blogs on the Internet, the bloggers, and their opinions
- **brick-and-mortar:** a company operating in a building or a store, not on the Internet
- **climate change:** changes in weather and temperature over a long period of time
- **go green:** take steps to reduce one's negative impact on the environment

*(See page 208 of the Independent Student Handbook for more information on building your vocabulary.)*

A *brick-and-mortar* store operates in a building, and not on the Internet.

Planting a tree is one way to *go green*.

1. **A:** Wow, another hot day! This must be the tenth in a row!
   **B:** I know! If you ask me, it's probably due to _____ . . .
2. **A:** Have you finished setting up your environmentalism blog yet?
   **B:** No, but I will soon. I'm really excited to enter _____ . . .
3. **A:** I sold my car and I'm only using a bicycle now. I'm also being careful to recycle everything that I can.
   **B:** Really? I can't believe it! You're the last person I thought would ever
   _____ . . .
4. **A:** Did you know that a new bookstore is opening downtown?
   **B:** Who cares? I buy all my books online. I have no use for _____ bookstores anymore.

# Grammar

*Ting*

## Verb + Gerund

Certain verbs can be followed by a *gerund* but not by an infinitive. A *gerund* is a word ending in *-ing*. Here are some verbs that can be followed by a *gerund*.

| | | | | |
|---|---|---|---|---|
| admit | appreciate | defend | enjoy | quit |
| avoid | be used to | deny | look forward to | risk |

*The king will not open up Bhutan all at once* **and risk ruining** *it.*
*We* **are looking forward to visiting** *the islands off Cornwall this summer.*

**A** | Read this article about the Amish people. <u>Underline</u> the verbs that are followed by a gerund.

An Amish man takes his horse-drawn carriage down a busy road.

The Amish people of the United States <u>enjoy</u> living simply. They <u>stop attending</u> school around the eighth grade, and they live without modern conveniences. The Amish <u>resist using</u> technologies such as electricity, automobiles, and computers. Many do not even <u>like having</u> their picture taken. Amish people are <u>accustomed to riding</u> in horse-drawn carriages. Most Amish people live in the states of Pennsylvania, Indiana, or Ohio. The average Amish family has five children.

The population of Amish people in the United States <u>keeps growing</u>. A recent survey counted 230,000 Amish people. Sixteen years ago, there were only about 115,000 Amish people. Older Amish communities no longer have enough land for their people. Although the Amish <u>recommend separating</u> oneself from the modern world, many can no longer <u>avoid going</u> out into the modern world to find a place to live. Rather than <u>risk living</u> near people who are not Amish, some Amish have moved far from their traditional homes to isolated areas of the United States and Canada.

**B** | **Collaboration.** Work with a partner. Use five of the verbs you found in exercise **A** to write sentences about your own feelings or experiences. Underline the verb + gerund in each sentence. Then share your sentences with a partner.

> I <u>enjoy giving</u> chocolate to my friends on Valentine's Day, but I hate chocolate myself.

# Interviewing a Classmate

**A** | Work with a partner. Your partner will choose a country or a city where he or she has lived. Interview your partner to determine the *Gross National Happiness* of the country or city. Read each question to your partner. Mark your partner's answer with a check (✔). Then switch roles.

| Gross National Happiness | Yes | No |
|---|---|---|
| **Pillar 1: Good Government** | | |
| 1. Does the government respond to the needs of the people? | | |
| 2. Does the government treat people fairly and with equality? | | |
| 3. Is the government's use of money, property, and other resources efficient? | | |
| **Pillar 2: Sustainable Development** | | |
| 1. Do most people enjoy their jobs? | | |
| 2. Do most jobs provide enough money to live on? | | |
| 3. Do most companies protect workers from dangerous working conditions? | | |
| **Pillar 3: Environmental Protection** | | |
| 1. Are levels of pollution, noise, and traffic acceptable? | | |
| 2. Are there parks or natural areas available to the public? | | |
| 3. Are there areas set aside for nature? | | |
| **Pillar 4: Cultural Preservation** | | |
| 1. Do people try to maintain traditions along with new practices? | | |
| 2. Are old buildings restored and valued? | | |
| 3. Do young people value and respect the older generations? | | |

**B** | **Discussion.** With your partner, discuss the questions from exercise **A**. Take notes on your partner's responses. If you answered *no* for any question, explain why you chose that answer.

**C** | Share your *Gross National Happiness* interviews with the class. Who in the class said *yes* to most questions? Who in the class said *no* to most questions? Talk about the answers with your class.

# Farm Restoration

The *Reinvest in Minnesota* project helps farmers return their farmlands to a natural state.

Okabena Creek, Minnesota

## Before Viewing

**A** | **Meaning from Context.** Read the sentences. Notice the words in blue. You will hear these words in the video.

1. I had an **epiphany**—it's more important to be happy than to be successful.
2. The area around Tintagel Castle in the United Kingdom experiences **erosion** as the sea takes more rock and soil each year.
3. When the actress died, she left 1000 acres of land for a wildlife reserve—a **legacy** for nature lovers to enjoy for many years in the future.
4. **Marginal** farmland is difficult to farm and does not produce a lot of crops.
5. During long, dry summers, many forests in California become **susceptible to** fire.
6. The flooding of the Mississippi River **took its toll** on riverside towns and washed away houses and farms.

**B** | **Using a Dictionary.** Match each word in blue from exercise **A** with its definition.

1. epiphany (n.)        _____    a.  land or money given to future generations
2. erosion (n.)         _____    b.  to have a bad effect or do a lot of damage
3. legacy (n.)          _____    c.  likely to be affected by
4. marginal (adj.)      _____    d.  a moment of sudden understanding
5. susceptible to (adj.) _____   e.  not very useful; on the edge of usefulness
6. took its toll (v.)   _____    f.  the removal of soil or rock by wind or water

# While Viewing

**A** | Watch the video. Then circle the correct answers.

1. What problem did Okabena Creek cause for farmer Dale Aden?
   a. There wasn't enough water in it for farming.
   b. It sometimes flooded part of his farmland.
   c. He couldn't use the water because it was polluted.
2. What was Dale Aden's epiphany about his marginal farmland?
   a. He realized that he could farm more corn and soybeans on it.
   b. He realized he could stop farming it if someone would buy it.
   c. He realized that he could return the land to wildlife.
3. What does the organization *Reinvest in Minnesota* do?
   a. It buys marginal farmland from farmers for wildlife.
   b. It helps farmers flood their land so people can't live there.
   c. It buys corn and soybeans to help farmers buy land.
4. What is Aden's marginal farmland used for today?
   a. It is used for farming only during dry years.
   b. It is returned to a natural state for wildlife to live on.
   c. Aden collects bird eggs from the farm to sell in markets.

**B** | Watch the video again. Complete the sentences with no more than three words from the video.

1. Aden said that he was a third _____ on this land.
2. For many years, Aden watched helplessly as _____ flooded its banks and soaked his crops.
3. Aden said that it takes _____ to pay for the lost crop.
4. Aden's friend planted prairie grass that will soon provide _____.
5. Aden calls the sound of birds singing "_____."
6. Aden couldn't be _____ for the way the project has turned out.

# After Viewing

**Critical Thinking.** Form a group with two or three other students. Discuss the questions.

1. The government program *Reinvest in Minnesota* pays farmers such as Dale Aden for their farmland. Do you think this program is a good idea? Why, or why not?
2. In this video, Dale Aden returned his land to a natural state. What are some possible positive and negative effects that this could have? Brainstorm these effects with your group.

Birds returned to the farmland once the land had been converted into a wildlife area.

**A** | **Using a Dictionary.** Check (✔) the words you already know. These are words you will hear and use in Lesson B. Then write each word from the box next to its definition. Use your dictionary to help you.

| | | | | |
|---|---|---|---|---|
| ❑ enable | ❑ found | ❑ highlight | ❑ perspective | ❑ regain |
| ❑ federal | ❑ grant | ❑ objective | ❑ portion | ❑ undertake |

1. _____ (v.) to give
2. _____ (v.) to establish or start
3. _____ (v.) to make possible
4. _____ (n.) a goal you are trying to achieve
5. _____ (n.) a way of thinking that is usually influenced by your own experiences
6. _____ (v.) to get something back that you had lost
7. _____ (v.) to emphasize or focus attention on
8. _____ (adj.) related to the central government of a country
9. _____ (n.) a part
10. _____ (v.) to start doing a task and accept responsibility for it

track 2-25 **B** | Read the interview and fill in each blank with the correct word from exercise **A**. Then listen and check your answers.

## Saving the World's Languages

**A:** What's happening to the world's languages?

**B:** Well, most people don't know that a language dies every 14 days. When a language dies, no one can speak the language anymore. National Geographic helped (1) _____ a project to save the world's most unique languages.

A Huilliche man plays a musical instrument he built.

**A:** How many languages are dying?

**B:** Scientists think that over half of the languages spoken today may no longer exist in 2100. In Chile, for example, the Huilliche language may die soon. Only a small (2) _____ of people can speak the language, and most of the speakers are over 70 years old.

**A:** Why does a language disappear?

**B:** There are many reasons. Governments sometimes create (3) _____ policies that tell citizens to speak only one language. Also, people may forget a language if they don't speak it often.

**A:** What made you (4) _____ the task of trying to save these languages?

**B:** Language is key to understanding how speakers think and communicate. Our (5) _____ is to help people keep their cultures alive. From my (6) _____ as a scientist, I think our work is very important.

**A:** What do you do to help groups (7) _____ dying languages?

**B:** We (8) _____ people to study their language by giving them recording devices. We make dictionaries, and we (9) _____ how people can teach their language to others. In the future, we can (10) _____ access to the recordings, so people can learn the language and keep it alive.

**A** | Complete the paragraph with the correct form of a word from the box.

| enable | federal | found | grant | portion | regain | undertake |

For many years, Native Americans in the United States have lived on reservations. Reservations are areas of land that were (1) _____ to the Native Americans by the (2) _____ government of the United States. The first reservations were (3) _____ as early as 1786. In its early history, the United States fought with many Native American groups, or tribes, and took away much of their land. Putting people on reservations (4) _____ the government to control the Native American groups more easily. On these reservations, Native Americans have often lived in poor economic conditions. In recent years, however, the situation has improved, and there are many successful Native American businesses on these reservations. Some Native American groups give a (5) _____ of the profits from the businesses to everyone in their group. The money has allowed them to (6) _____ projects to improve their reservations. Some groups are using their money to buy back some of their original lands. Government records show that Native Americans have (7) _____ nearly a million acres of land in this way.

Native American groups wear traditional clothing at a celebration.

**B** | **Choosing the Right Definition.** Study the numbered definitions for objective. Write the number of the definition next to the correct sentence below.

> **objective** /əbdʒɛktɪv/ **(objectives)** [1] N-COUNT Your **objective** is what you are trying to achieve. • *Their objective was to preserve Native American traditions.* [2] ADJ **Objective** information is based on facts. • *A scientist is concerned with objective facts, not opinions.* [3] ADJ If a person is **objective**, they base their opinions on facts rather than on their personal feelings. • *He loves his children so much that he can't be objective when he talks about them.*

_____ a. Try not to take sides in the argument and maybe you can remain objective.

_____ b. His objective was to learn as many Native American languages as possible.

_____ c. It's an objective truth that humans lived in Yellowstone 11,000 years ago.

**C** | **Discussion.** Form a group with two or three other students. Read the statements. Do you agree or disagree with each statement? Share your opinions with your group.

1. Schools should highlight the role of the U.S. government in taking away Native American lands.

2. From my perspective, Native Americans should not live separated on reservations. Instead, they should live with the general American population.

## Before Listening

 **Prior Knowledge.** With a partner, look at the map and answer the questions.

1. Read the names of the Native American groups. Have you heard of any of these Native American groups on the map? If so, what do you know about them?
2. What are some other Native American groups that you have heard about?

## Listening: A Study Group Discussion

track 2-26 **A** | **Listening for Main Ideas.** Listen to a group of classmates reviewing for an exam. Then choose the correct answers.

1. What is the main topic of the conversation?
   a. The poor condition of Native American reservation land
   b. How Native Americans are restoring their lands to their original condition
   c. Conflicts over land ownership between Native Americans and European Americans

2. Originally, what was the attitude of the United States government toward Native American culture and traditions?
   a. The government wanted to change them.
   b. The government was sorry for damaging them.
   c. The government supported them.

3. According to the conversation, what is an important source of revenue for the Native Americans?
   a. Donations from people who support their cause
   b. Money provided by the United States government
   c. Revenue from businesses on their reservations

### Critical Thinking Focus: Evaluating Numbers and Statistics

When you hear a speaker say a number or statistic, try to evaluate the number by asking yourself questions. For example:

*Is this a large or a small number?*          *What percentage of the total is it?*
*Is it larger or smaller than I expected?*     *Does this number seem accurate?*

**B | Note-Taking.** Listen again and complete the notes.

track 2-26

**Background**

> 300 Native American _____ in the U.S.

U.S. forced them to adopt _____

Most reservations located _____ of Miss.
Land not suitable for _____

1970: U.S. granted right to run various _____
Used money to _____

**InterTribal Sinkyone Wilderness Area**

Founded on the _____, north of San Francisco

Access very _____

Gather food, have religious _____ here

**Big Cypress Swamp**

Owned by the Seminole group in _____

Bringing back _____ that used to live there

Removing _____ that weren't there originally

The InterTribal Sinkyone Wilderness Area

## After Listening

**Discussion.** With a partner, discuss the questions.

1. Describe the Native American relationship with nature. Does your culture have any traditions or beliefs related to nature? Explain.
2. The Native Americans are removing animals from the Big Cypress Swamp that were not there originally. How did these animals get into the swamp? Share your ideas with your partner.

## Pronunciation

 **Linking Consonants to Vowels**

track 2-27

When a word ends in a consonant sound and the next word begins with a vowel sound, the two words are linked so that they sound like one word. Linking can occur in strings of two or more words.

*turn off*          *deer and other animals*

 **A |** Listen to the six words and linked phrases. Then listen again and repeat.

track 2-28

 **B |** Practice saying the sentences with a partner. Mark the linked words as in the example.
Then listen and check your pronunciation.

track 2-29

1. Click on the file to open it.
2. You should speak out again.
3. He doesn't have an opinion.
4. The car dealer made an offer.
5. This car is new and improved.
6. Land conservation isn't easy.

## Language Function

### Expressing a Lack of Knowledge

In conversation, you often hear things that you didn't know about before. You can use the following expressions to explain that a certain fact is new to you.

*I had no idea (that) . . .*          *I didn't realize (that) . . .*
*I never knew (that) . . .*          *I wasn't aware (that) . . .*

track 2-30 **A** | In the study group discussion, the speakers expressed a lack of knowledge. Listen to the sentences and fill in the expressions.

1. **Amina:** _____ there are more than 300 Native American reservations in the United States, did you?
   **Jose:** No, I definitely didn't. And _____ the reservations only make up two percent of the total land area of the United States.

2. **Lauren:** For a long time the people who lived there lived in bad economic conditions.
   **Jose:** _____. So, when did things begin to get better?

 **B** | Read the beginnings of these newspaper articles. Use the expressions from the Language Function box to tell a partner about the information that is new to you. Discuss other things you know or would like to know about each topic.

### Olmec Stone Carvings Discovered

A giant stone carving of three cats was recently discovered in Mexico. The carvings are believed to be the work of the Olmec people. The Olmec people lived in Mexico and Central America between 1200 and 400 BC.

### New Theories about Machu Picchu

Machu Picchu is a unique place high in the mountains of Peru. It has ruins[1] of structures built by the Inca people. It is one of the most popular tourist destinations in the world. There are various theories about Machu Picchu's purpose, but nobody knows for sure why it was built. Some theories say it was a religious place, but some scientists now believe that it was the home of the Incan king.

[1] **Ruins** of a building are parts that remain after the building has fallen down.

> I had no idea that the Olmec people carved cats in stone.

> Neither did I. I wonder what else they carved.

# Grammar

## Verb + Object + Infinitive

Some verbs can be followed by an object and an *infinitive*. An *infinitive* consists of *to* + verb.
> *Their prosperity **is allowing them to save** a part of the Big Cypress Swamp.*

The verbs in this list are usually followed by an infinitive. Some of them are followed by an object and an infinitive.

| | | | | | | |
|---|---|---|---|---|---|---|
| *advise* | *ask* | *forbid* | *invite* | *permit* | *remind* | *warn* |
| *allow* | *encourage* | *force* | *order* | *persuade* | *tell* | |

> *She **asked me to invite** her brother to the party.*
> *I **will encourage him to open** his own business.*

To form the negative, insert *not* before the infinitive:
> *The guide **reminded us not to enter** the reservation without permission.*

**A** | **Collaboration.** With a partner, write four statements using the verb + object + infinitive pattern. Use the verbs from the list in the box above.

1. *Victor persuaded his friend to move to the city.* _____
2. _____
3. _____
4. _____
5. _____

**B** | **Self-Reflection.** Work with your partner. Talk about people or events that have influenced your life. Use the verbs from the grammar box and the verb + object + infinitive pattern while speaking.

> My parents always encouraged me to go to college.

> That's great. Did you follow their advice?

## Presentation Skills: Varying your Voice Volume

*Volume* means the loudness or softness of your voice. When speaking to a partner or a small group, you can use your regular, everyday volume level. However, for larger groups and class presentations, your everyday voice can sound too quiet. For presentations, you will need to increase your volume. You can also introduce excitement into your voice by varying the volume. Emphasize some words by saying them more loudly than others. Create drama by lowering your voice as well. Varying your volume will help keep your audience interested during conversations and presentations.

# 6

You may have to do research on the Internet for class or work. However, information found on the Internet isn't always reliable. Anyone can create a Web site, and while some Web sites are created by experts, most are not. When you want to use information from a Web site in a presentation or paper, it is necessary to evaluate the Web site. Web sites should contain accurate and objective information and be free of *bias*. Bias is an unfair opinion about a group or idea.

**A** | Do an Internet search about a popular tradition in a country of your choice. Select a Web site from the search results. Evaluate the Web site and complete the form below.

### Web Site Evaluation Form

Search Topic: _____ Name of Site: _____

Web Address: _____

1. Who is the author of the Web site?
   - ❏ Author unknown
   - ❏ Author's name _____
   - ❏ Author's qualifications (if available) _____

2. Is there contact information for the author or the Web site owner on the site?
   - ❏ Yes        ❏ No

3. What is the suffix on the Web site address?
   - ❏ .gov        ❏ .com        ❏ .edu        ❏ Other: _____

4. What is the general purpose of the Web site?
   - ❏ scholarly        ❏ educational        ❏ entertainment
   - ❏ to give an opinion        ❏ to sell something

5. When was information posted or last updated? _____

6. How does the site look?
   - ❏ well-maintained        ❏ out-of-date

7. Is the site easy to use?
   - ❏ Yes        ❏ No

8. Does the Web site include advertisements?
   - ❏ Yes        ❏ No        ❏ If yes, what kind? _____

**B** | Imagine that you had to write a paper about the topic you selected. With a partner, discuss your Web site. Decide if each Web site is an appropriate and reliable source to use in your paper. Explain what makes your Web site a good source or a poor source.

**C** | With your partner, join another pair of students. Each group member will present his or her Web site to the group. Use your form to explain your Web site. As a group, rank the Web sites from the most reliable to the least reliable.

# Money in Our Lives

ACADEMIC PATHWAYS

Lesson A:  Listening to a Radio Interview
Discussing Values

Lesson B:  Listening to a Conversation between Friends
Preparing a Budget

## Think and Discuss

1. What is happening in this photo? Read the caption. Does this activity surprise you?

2. An old saying goes, "Love of money is the root of all evil." Does this saying seem true to you? Explain.

Friends pin money to a man's suit during his birthday party in New Orleans, Louisiana.

# Exploring the Theme:
## Money in Our Lives

Look at the photos and the chart and read the captions. Then discuss the questions.

1. Which country in the chart has the largest public debt per person? Which country has the smallest? Does any of the information in this chart surprise you?
2. What are some of the ways that money can affect people's happiness?
3. Twenty years from now, how do you imagine you will pay for most things?

### Electronic Money

Today, electronic money such as credit and debit cards is replacing paper money. Many experts predict that the world will one day have a cashless economy.

### Money and Happiness

As part of a yearly tradition, a girl gives a child money in a red envelope. Scientists are studying money to see how it affects our lives and our happiness.

### Public Debt Per Person

Brazil, $5668
China, $922
United States, $37,953
Kenya, $394
Japan, $87,600
Russia, $1253
Spain $17,539
Singapore, $43,191
Italy, $38,026
Turkey, $4498
United Kingdom $32,208

Source: The Economist

Many governments spend more money than they have. *Public debt* is money that is owed by a government. Unfortunately, public debt is growing. When debt gets too high, it can threaten the economy of a country.

In Hong Kong, stacks of fake money are for sale.

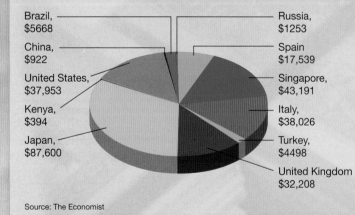

track **3-2** **A** | **Meaning from Context.** Read and listen to the paragraphs. Notice the words in blue. These are the words you will hear and use in Lesson A.

Credit card debt is a major problem in the United States, as these statistics show:

- The average debt per household is reported to be about $15,799.

- Unpaid credit card bills in a recent year totaled around 69 billion dollars.

Kelly Jones got herself in debt by using 10 credit cards, but she recently ceased using them completely. To pay off her $15,000 debt, Jones works 64 hours a week at two jobs. She started a debt-management plan, and hopes to pay off her bills in seven years. She will no longer purchase unnecessary items. "I have no idea what I bought. I have nothing to show for it," she says. Now, Jones warns young people not to repeat her errors, and tells them about what can happen if they rely on credit cards too much.

A financial counselor[1] sorts through thousands of pieces of cut-up credit cards. Obviously, these cards won't be used again. Counselors ask people who are in debt to cut up all of their credit cards. This is just one component of a process to help clients[2] pay their bills. Counselors display the cut-up cards to demonstrate that people are not alone. Cutting up credit cards shows the commitment that hundreds of people have made to control their spending. Each year millions of people seek help to get out of debt. Many of these people receive counseling and education to promote better money management.

[1]A **counselor** gives information and support to people who need help.
[2]A **client** is a person who receives a service from a company or professional.

**B** | Write each word in blue from exercise **A** next to its definition.

1. _____ (v.) stopped
2. _____ (v.) to show
3. _____ (v.) to buy
4. _____ (n.) one part, which together with other parts makes a whole
5. _____ (v.) to advance, encourage, or improve
6. _____ (adv.) clearly; used when something is said that is already understood
7. _____ (n.) mistakes
8. _____ (adj.) extremely important
9. _____ (n.) a promise to complete a task
10. _____ (n.) information in the form of numbers

**A** | Complete each sentence with the correct form of a word from the box.

| cease | error | obviously | promote | purchase | statistics |

1. _____ things you want can make you happy for a short time, but the feeling doesn't last very long.

2. One common _____ people make is spending money on items they don't need.

3. Spending money on others _____ happiness more than spending money on oneself.

4. My car is still being repaired, so _____ I will need to take the bus to work.

5. According to government _____, people making over $100,000 a year spend almost 20 percent of their time on relaxing activities such as watching TV and visiting friends.

6. British philosopher John Stuart Mill said, "Ask yourself whether you are happy and you _____ to be so."

**B** | **Discussion.** With a partner, discuss the questions.

1. "Happiness requires your emotional **commitment** to your career." What do you think this statement means? Do you agree or disagree with it? Explain.

2. Can you think of a movie, play, or story that **demonstrates** the theme that money doesn't buy happiness? Explain how it demonstrates that theme.

3. Most people would agree that having money is a **component** of happiness. What are some of the other components of a happy life? Give examples.

**C** | **Choosing the Right Definition.** Study the numbered definitions for the word major. Write the number of the definition next to the correct sentence below.

> **major** /ˈmeɪdʒər/ **(majors, majoring, majored)** [1] ADJ You use **major** when you want to describe something that is more important, serious, or significant than other things in a group or situation. • *Unemployment is a major problem for workers and the economy.* [2] N-COUNT At a university or college, a student's **major** is the main subject that he or she is studying. • *I need to choose a major by the end of my second year.* [3] V-I If a student at a university or college **majors in** a particular subject, that subject is the main one he or she studies. • *I'm majoring in biology at Northwestern University.*

_____ a. Why don't you choose a major that will be useful to your career?

_____ b. They made some major changes to their spending habits to get out of debt.

_____ c. I want to make a lot of money, so I'm planning to major in business.

## Before Listening

**A** | Read the statements about money. How happy does each situation make you? Rank them from 1 (the happiest) to 5 (the least happy).

_____ Having money in the bank

_____ Spending money on items you want

_____ Giving money to other people

_____ Earning money

_____ Receiving money as a gift

 **B** | **Discussion.** Form a group with two or three other students. Compare and discuss your rankings from exercise **A**. Then come up with a new ranking list for your group. Take a group vote on which item should be ranked number 1 and so on.

## Listening: A Radio Interview

track 3-3 **A** | **Listening for Main Ideas.** Listen to a radio interview about money and happiness. Then choose the correct answer for each question.

1. What does a recent study by psychologist Elizabeth Dunn show?
   a. Spending money brings us more happiness than saving money.
   b. Spending money on others brings us more happiness than spending it on ourselves.
   c. Possessions bring us more happiness than experiences.

2. What caused Dunn to research the relationship between money and happiness?
   a. She had more money and wanted to know how to use it.
   b. She lost her job as a professor and needed to live on less money.
   c. Her university asked her to study student happiness levels.

3. What common error do people make when they try to buy happiness with money?
   a. They are afraid to buy the things that will really make them happy.
   b. They think major purchases such as houses will make them happy.
   c. They use scientific research instead of their own feelings when spending money.

4. In their study, what question did Leaf Van Boven and Tom Gilovich want to answer?
   a. Does having money in the bank make people happier than spending it?
   b. Does spending money on things help people think of themselves differently?
   c. Does money spent on experiences make people happier than money spent on items?

5. What did Angus Deaton and Daniel Kahneman's study reveal?
   a. Making more than a certain amount of money causes unhappiness.
   b. Making more than a certain amount of money doesn't affect happiness much.
   c. Making more than a certain amount of money causes greater happiness.

**B** | **Note-Taking.** Listen again and complete the outline with information from the radio interview. (*See page 206 of the Independent Student Handbook for more information on note-taking.*)

---

Happiness Studies

I. Elizabeth Dunn

    A. Research question: Do people get more happiness from spending money on themselves or _____?

    B. Experiment:

        1. Gave people _____

        2. Asked some people to spend it _____, others _____

        3. At end of day, _____

    C. Result: _____

II. Leaf van Boven & Tom Gilovich

    A. Research question: What is the value of spending money on _____ versus _____?

    B. Experiment: _____

    C. Result: _____

III. Angus Deaton & Daniel Kahneman

    A. Research question: Does more money = _____?

    B. Experiment: _____

    C. Result: _____

---

# After Listening

## Critical Thinking Focus: Summarizing

A summary is a shortened version of a text or listening passage that contains all of the main ideas and a few important details. A summary usually includes (1) a general opening statement, (2) the main ideas, and (3) a concluding statement. The parts of the summary should be connected with transitions. A summary can be written or oral, and it should not include your opinion.

**A** | **Summarizing.** Work with two other students. Use your notes from exercise **B** above to summarize the studies on money and happiness. Each student should summarize one study. (*See page 206 of the Independent Student Handbook for more information on summarizing*)

**B** | **Discussion.** With your group, discuss the questions.

1. Elizabeth Dunn's study shows that giving money away makes people happier than spending it on themselves. Why do you think this is true?
2. Compare a time when you spent money on an experience with a time when you bought an item you wanted. Which purchase made you happier? Explain.

# Language Function

## Showing That You Are Following a Conversation

There are a number of useful expressions for showing that you are following or understanding someone while they are speaking to you.

*I see.*

*Oh!*

*Uh-huh.* (Use with rising intonation.)

*Really?* (Use with falling intonation.)

*Is that so?* (Use with falling intonation.)

*Is it? Are you? Did they?* (These are tag questions with falling intonation.)

track 3-4 **A** | In the radio interview, the interviewer used a number of expressions to show that he was following the conversation. Listen and fill in the missing expressions.

1. **Dr. Simmons:** That's what Dunn said in a recent interview with National Geographic.

   **Dave Martin:** _____? How did she discover that?

2. **Dr. Simmons:** So, Dr. Dunn decided to do some scientific research to see if people might get more happiness from using their money to help other people, rather than themselves.

   **Dave Martin:** _____. And how did she research this topic?

3. **Dr. Simmons:** Since then, Dr. Dunn has completed a lot of other research on money and happiness.

   **Dave Martin:** _____?

4. **Dr. Simmons:** Actually, there are no statistics to prove that owning a home makes people happy.

   **Dave Martin:** _____. Are there other studies relating money and happiness?

**B** | Read the questions and complete the survey.

How worried are you about . . .

| | Very | Somewhat | Slightly | Not at all |
|---|---|---|---|---|
| the world economy? | ❑ | ❑ | ❑ | ❑ |
| getting a job? | ❑ | ❑ | ❑ | ❑ |
| keeping your job? | ❑ | ❑ | ❑ | ❑ |
| personal debt? | ❑ | ❑ | ❑ | ❑ |
| national debt? | ❑ | ❑ | ❑ | ❑ |
| increasing food prices? | ❑ | ❑ | ❑ | ❑ |
| increasing fuel prices? | ❑ | ❑ | ❑ | ❑ |
| crime? | ❑ | ❑ | ❑ | ❑ |

**C** | **Discussion.** Work with a partner. Choose three of your responses to the survey on page 128 and explain them to your partner. Give reasons why you chose each answer.

> I'm worried about getting a job. I've been looking for one for a while now.

> Have you? What kind of job are you looking for?

 **D** | **Critical Thinking.** Form a group with two or three other students. Recently, the Nielsen Company gave the survey on page 128 to hundreds of people around the world. Look at the photo below and read the caption. How do you think people in other parts of the world answered this survey? Use the expressions from the Language Function box on page 128 in your discussion.

In the Asia-Pacific area, people are the most worried about rising food prices.

# Grammar

## Using Connectors to Add and Emphasize Information

Connectors are words and phrases to add or emphasize information while we speak.

To join similar ideas, use *and*, *also*, *as well as*, or *both . . . and . . . .*
> Some people spend money on other people, **and** some spend it on themselves.
> I have a checking account. I **also** have a savings account.
> I have **both** a checking account **and** a savings account.

To add information and emphasize it, use *not only . . . but also . . . .*
> We've **not only** cut out any short trips, **but also** cancelled our yearly vacation.

To emphasize a sentence, use *furthermore*, *what's more*, *in fact*, or *actually*.
> Buying a home is too expensive for me right now. **In fact**, I'll probably rent forever.
> I love my job because the work is fun. **What's more**, my office is near my house.

👥 **Understanding Visuals.** Work with a partner. Study the graphs. With your partner, answer the questions about the graphs. Use connectors from page 129 when possible.

1. What do these graphs show? Explain one of the graphs to your partner.

> Around 23 percent of people in Latin America are cutting down on take-out meals. Also, 14 percent are using their cars less often.

2. How do you spend your extra money? How does your spending compare with the world average?

3. How will you save your money in the future? Talk about the habits from the graphs that you think are useful.

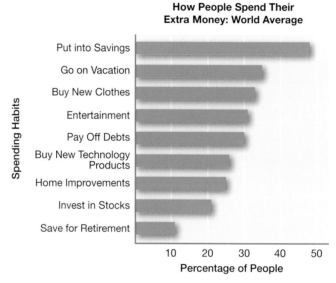

**How People Spend Their Extra Money: World Average**

Source: The Nielsen Company, Global Online Survey, 2010

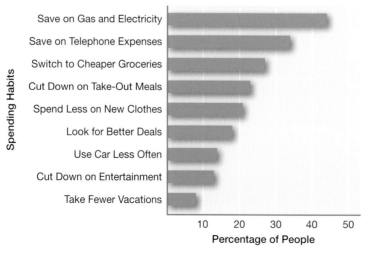

**Spending Habits People Will Continue After the Economy Improves: Latin America**

Source: The Nielsen Company, Global Online Survey, 2010

# Discussing Values

The *values* of a person or group are the beliefs that they think are important. Your personal experiences, family and friends, and education can help you choose your values. Some examples of values are respect for others, honesty, friendliness, and kindness.

**A** | List the most expensive items, services, or experiences that you have ever purchased. Then list the items, services, or experiences that gave the most happiness. Circle the items that are on both lists.

| Expensive List | Happiness List |
| --- | --- |
| 1. _____ | 1. _____ |
| 2. _____ | 2. _____ |
| 3. _____ | 3. _____ |
| 4. _____ | 4. _____ |
| 5. _____ | 5. _____ |
| 6. _____ | 6. _____ |
| 7. _____ | 7. _____ |
| 8. _____ | 8. _____ |

**B** | Work with a partner and compare your lists. Explain why the items on your Happiness list made you happy. Take turns asking and answering questions about interesting items on your partner's lists.

> Tell me about your watch. Why does it make you happy?

> I love it because it was a gift from my grandfather.

**C** | **Critical Thinking.** With your partner, discuss the questions.

1. What are some of your personal values? How does money relate to your personal values? Explain.
2. Scientists believe that spending money on experiences makes us happier than spending money on items. Based on your lists from exercise **A**, do you agree with this? Explain.
3. What conclusions can you make about what makes you happy from the information in your lists? Explain this to your partner.

**Student to Student:**
**Asking Sensitive Questions**

Some people are uncomfortable talking about sensitive topics such as money, death, or family issues. If you must ask a question about a sensitive topic, use one of these expressions to make your partner feel more comfortable.

*Do you mind if I ask you . . . ?*
*Excuse me for asking, but . . . ?*
*If you don't mind my asking . . . ?*

# The Black Diamonds of Provence

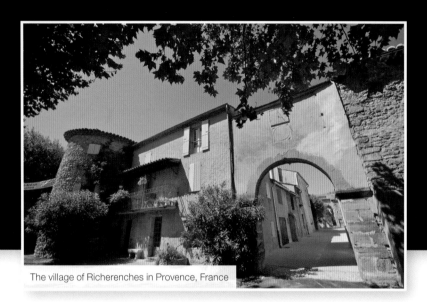

The village of Richerenches in Provence, France

## Before Viewing

**A | Using the Dictionary.** You will hear these words in the video. Match each word with its definition. Use your dictionary to help you.

1. discreetly (adj.) _____   a. a businessman who sets up purchases and sales
2. lucrative (adj.) _____   b. easily affected by small amounts of something
3. broker (n.) _____   c. to sell products and materials to another country
4. export (v.) _____   d. profitable; making a lot of money
5. sensitive (adj.) _____   e. carefully; quietly

**B | Predicting Content.** You are going to watch a video about finding, buying, and selling truffles. Why do you think truffles are expensive? Share your ideas with a partner.

## While Viewing

**A |** Watch the video. Then circle the correct answer to each question.

Black truffles are an expensive delicacy.

1. What do many truffle hunters do in winter?
   a. Take a vacation
   b. Work on their farms
   c. Sell truffles
2. Why do truffle brokers sell and buy truffles for cash?
   a. To avoid taxes
   b. To do business faster
   c. To control the price of truffles

3. What are truffles used for?
   a. Simple family meals
   b. Expensive gourmet dishes
   c. A few traditional French dishes
4. What problem do truffle hunters and brokers have today?
   a. The price of truffles is falling rapidly.
   b. The demand for truffles is declining.
   c. There aren't as many truffles as there used to be.

**B** | **Note-Taking.** Watch the video again. Complete the notes with information from the video.

Richerenches:

• a town in _____, in southern France

• has one of the largest _____ in France

Truffles:

• are black with _____ veins

• are used a lot in France, _____, and _____

Possible reasons for decline:

• _____

• _____

Dogs:

• have sensitive _____

• can _____ truffles

# After Viewing

**Critical Thinking.** Form a group with two or three other students. Discuss the questions.

1. Why do you think truffles are called "black diamonds"? Give evidence to support your answer.
2. Look again at the possible reasons for decline that you wrote in While Viewing, exercise **B**. What other possible reasons could there be for fewer truffles?
3. In Before Viewing, exercise **B**, you discussed why truffles are expensive. Was your answer correct? Now that you have watched the video, write a new answer to the question that includes more information. Share your answer with the group.

The black truffle is a type of *fungus*—a plant that has no flowers, leaves, or green coloring.

track 3-5   **A** | **Meaning from Context.** Read and listen to the interview. Notice the words in blue. These are the words you will hear and use in Lesson B.

**Q:** The world's financial crisis shows that the way individuals manage their money can affect the whole world. Still, many people are unsure of how the crisis began. I'm speaking with economist Ken Lonoff. Mr. Lonoff, where did the crisis begin?

**A:** It began in the United States. As you know, most people want to buy their own home, but very few people can pay in paper currency— cash, that is. Banks have to help these consumers by loaning them money to buy things. People need to meet certain criteria to get a loan. For example, they need to have a job and be able to pay their bills.

A man reacts to sudden changes in the stock market.

**Q:** So, how exactly did this crisis begin?

**A:** Well, in the years that preceded the crisis, the economy was good. Financial professionals made as many loans as they could and earned a fee for each one. They were happy to assist anyone who wanted a loan. Even people without jobs were capable of getting loans. A huge number of these loans were made.

**Q:** When did things start to go wrong?

**A:** Things started to go wrong in 2007, when many people could not pay back their loans. These loans were the foundation for many businesses in the United States and all over the world. Huge sums were lost, and many companies went out of business. Loans became very difficult to get, and as a result, economies of countries around the world were affected.

**B** | Write the correct word in blue from exercise **A** to complete each definition.

1. _____ are people with special training in a job or career.

2. The money and coins used in a country are its _____.

3. _____ of money are amounts of money.

4. A group of people is made up of many _____.

5. _____ are people who buy things or pay for services.

6. An event that happened before another _____ it.

7. _____ are the factors used to judge or decide something.

8. A _____ is the money paid to a person or organization for a service.

9. If you are _____ of completing a task, you are able to do it.

10. When you help a person, you _____ them.

**A** | Read the personal finance tips below. Complete each sentence with the correct form of a word from the box.

| assist | capable | consumer | fee | precede | professional | sum |
|--------|---------|----------|-----|---------|--------------|-----|

---

## Personal Finance Tips

- Pay the most important bills first. Payment of overdue bills should (1) _____ payment of bills that are not late yet.

- Always pay your bills on time. That way, you will avoid unnecessary late (2) _____ .

- Set up your bank account so that a certain (3) _____ is automatically moved to a savings account each month. It's a good way to force yourself to save money.

- For questions about investing money, insurance, or taxes, be sure to hire a financial (4) _____ . They have the knowledge and training to (5) _____ you with your questions. Do not rely solely on the advice of family and friends.

- Always keep some money available for emergencies. You should be (6) _____ of living on your savings for at least three months if you lose your job.

- Smart (7) _____ compare prices before buying an item. Before you pay a price that is too high, check the prices at other stores and on the Internet.

---

**B** | **Discussion.** With a partner, discuss the questions.

1. Which of the above Personal Financial Tips have you followed in your life? If you were a financial **professional**, what suggestions would you give to a person who wanted to save money?

2. Think of a major purchase you made in the past year. What **criteria** did you use to choose that item?

3. How much money do you think an **individual** spends during his or her life? Explain why you chose the number you did.

4. Do you think that the entire world should use one **currency**? Why, or why not?

## Before Listening

 Read about these three types of payment cards. With a partner, discuss the questions that follow.

### Three Types of Payment Cards

**Debit Cards:** Debit cards are directly connected to the money in your bank account. When you use your debit card, money is immediately taken out of your account.

**Credit Cards:** When you use a credit card, you are borrowing money. The credit card company makes the payment for you and you must pay the money back. If you don't make your payments on time, you can be charged late fees. A *charge card* is a specific type of credit card. The main difference is that you must always pay your balance in full each month.

**Stored-Value Cards:** Stored-value cards have electronic money stored right on the card. Anyone can use these cards, not just the person who originally bought the card. Examples are prepaid phone cards and gift cards.

1. Which of these payment cards do you use? How often do you use them?
2. What other methods of payment do you regularly use?

## Listening: A Conversation between Friends

 track 3-6 **A** | **Listening for Main Ideas.** Listen to three people talking about money. Then circle the correct answer to each question.

1. Where are the people?
   a. At a restaurant
   b. At an ATM
   c. At work
2. What payment cards do the speakers use the most?
   a. Credit cards
   b. Debit and stored-value cards
   c. Debit and credit cards
3. According to Tina, why are credit cards dangerous?
   a. They're easy to steal or copy.
   b. They contain the owner's personal information.
   c. It's easy to get into debt if you have a credit card.
4. What is the problem with stored-value cards?
   a. There is a limit on how much value they can have.
   b. If they're lost, their value cannot be replaced.
   c. They are very expensive to buy.
5. Which statement about peer-to-peer lending is correct?
   a. It allows people to borrow from banks more easily.
   b. It is used mostly for large international loans.
   c. It allows individuals to loan money directly to other individuals.

Walter Cavanagh is known as "Mr. Plastic Fantastic." He holds the world record for the largest credit card collection—over 1400 working cards.

**B | Listening for Details.** Listen again. According to the speakers, are these statements true or false? Circle **T** for *true* or **F** for *false*.

| | | | |
|---|---|---|---|
| 1. | Debit cards preceded credit cards. | **T** | **F** |
| 2. | Peer-to-peer lending services are managed by banks. | **T** | **F** |
| 3. | Peer-to-peer lending services allow international loans. | **T** | **F** |
| 4. | James is going to pay for lunch. | **T** | **F** |

## After Listening

**Discussion.** With a partner, discuss the questions.

1. Would you like to get involved in borrowing or lending through peer-to-peer loans? Explain.
2. How often do you visit a bank? What is a typical experience at a bank like for you?

## Pronunciation

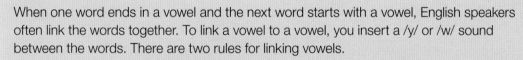

**Vowel-to-Vowel Linking**

When one word ends in a vowel and the next word starts with a vowel, English speakers often link the words together. To link a vowel to a vowel, you insert a /y/ or /w/ sound between the words. There are two rules for linking vowels.

1. When the first word ends in the sound /iy/, /ey/, /ay/, or /oy/, insert /y/:
   *happy ending* → **happy /y/ ending**
   *hardly ever*     *nearly everything*        *see it*          *the end*

2. When the first word ends in the sound /uw/, /ow/, or /aw/, insert /w/:
   *do over* → **do /w/ over**
   *Do you ever*     *go online*          *do it*          *so easy*

**A |** Work with a partner. Practice saying the phrases below. Insert a /y/ or /w/ into the phrases, according to the rules from the Pronunciation box. Then listen to check your pronunciation.

1. be __/y/__ able
2. the value _____ of
3. Do _____ it again.
4. Say _____ it in English.

5. nearly _____ all
6. the _____ answer
7. Who _____ ate it?
8. want to _____ understand

**B | Self-Reflection.** With your partner, answer the questions. Focus on vowel-to-vowel linking.

1. Do you ever buy things you don't need? Give an example.
2. What was the last movie you watched in a movie theater? Did you stay until the end?
3. How many times do you go online every day?
4. Why are you studying English?

## Language Function

**Digressing from the Topic**

Sometimes, in the middle of a conversation, we suddenly want to talk about a new topic. *Digressing* means talking about a new or different topic. Here are some expressions we can use to signal that we are bringing up a new topic.

If something the other person said made you think of the new topic, say:
  *Speaking of . . .*                    *That reminds me . . .*

If a new topic enters your head suddenly, but is not being discussed, say:
  *Incidentally . . .*                    *By the way . . .*

track 3-9

**A** | In the conversation on page 136, you heard two useful expressions for digressing from the topic. Listen to the sentences and fill in the missing expressions.

  1. **Tina:** _____, here's a trivia question for you. Which came first: the credit card or the debit card?

  2. **James:** _____, I read about an interesting way of borrowing and lending money. It's called peer-to-peer lending.

**B** | **Discussion.** With a partner, discuss one of the topics below. Look at the possible digressions from the topic. As you talk about the topic, digress from the topic when you have an idea that you would like to talk about.

| Topic #1: Taking out a loan |
| --- |
| **Possible Digressions:** |
| You discovered an interesting new store. |
| You want to find a higher-paying job. |

| Topic #2: Giving money to charity |
| --- |
| **Possible Digressions:** |
| You donated old clothes to charity. |
| You bought a new smart phone. |

I've been thinking about taking out a loan to buy a new car.

Really?

Yes, I'm tired of driving such an old car.

That reminds me, I heard that there's a new way to get loans over the Internet.

# Grammar

## Using Connectors of Concession

We use connectors to show a relationship between two statements. *Concession* is a special type of contrast. We use concession to show the differences between two statements, or to explain information that is surprising or unexpected.

To connect clauses, use *yet*.
> *Money is only paper,* **yet** *most people spend their entire lives trying to get more of it.*

Within a sentence, use *although, even*, or *though*.
> **Although** *Loretta worked for ten hours, she didn't finish her project.*

Between sentences, use *even so, nonetheless*, or *nevertheless*.
> *The loan I received was small.* **Even so,** *it made a huge difference in my life.*

**A** | **Collaboration.** Read the sentences. With a partner, match the sentences that go together. Then use connectors and combine each pair of sentences. Write as many different sentences as you can.

1. My boss knows I need a raise. _____f_____
2. The government is printing a lot of money. _____
3. I'm trying to find a job. _____
4. Almost everyone wants to be a millionaire. _____
5. Mary donates a lot of money to charity. _____
6. I bought a small house to save money. _____

a. Money can't buy happiness.
b. She doesn't make much money herself.
c. I could have bought a bigger one.
d. It isn't creating any jobs.
e. I'm not having any luck.
f. She refuses to give me one.

A man works on a money-printing machine in Germany.

**B** | **Discussion.** With your partner, look at the sentences you wrote in exercise **A**. Have a conversation about each topic.

> I just bought a house a few months ago.

> That's great. What does it look like?

# ENGAGE: Preparing a Budget

You will role-play a meeting between a financial professional and a client to discuss ways that the client can save money. With your partner, you will prepare a budget and present it to your classmates.

 **A** | Work with a partner. Read the role cards and choose your role.

### Role #1: Financial Professional

You are a financial professional. Discuss the client's budget with him or her, ask questions, and offer suggestions for reducing expenses and increasing savings.

### Role #2: Client

You recently moved into a new home and now your expenses are more than your income. Explain the problem and ask about ways to reduce your expenses.

 **B** | **Role-Playing.** Study the client's monthly budget and discuss the questions with your partner. Work with your partner and write a budget plan so that the client's income is more than his or her expenses. Also include a plan for how to repay the client's debt.

1. What is the difference between income and expenses? Use your dictionary to help you.
2. Which expenses cannot be changed?
3. On which items do you think the client needs to spend more money?
4. On which items do you think the client should spend less money?
5. Which loan should the client pay back first? Explain.

| Income: | $3200 | Expenses: | | Debts: | |
|---|---|---|---|---|---|
| Savings: | $ 0 | Rent: | $1040 | Student loan: (2% interest for 15 years) | $10,500 |
| | | Food: | $ 300 | | |
| | | Heat and Electricity: | $ 200 | | |
| | | Gas for Car: | $ 120 | | |
| | | Entertainment: | $ 425 | Car loan balance: (4% interest for 4 years) | $ 4600 |
| | | Health insurance: | $ 450 | | |
| | | Charity donation: | $ 100 | | |
| | | Credit card payment: | $ 400 | Credit card balance: (18% interest per year) | $ 1290 |
| | | Student loan payment: | $ 100 | | |
| | | Car loan payment: | $ 140 | | |
| Total Income: $3200 | | Total Expenses: | $3275 | Total Debt: | $16,390 |

 **C** | **Presentation.** With your partner from exercise **B**, present your budget plan to another pair of students. Then compare the plans. How were they similar? How were they different?

## Presentation Skills: Dealing with Difficult Questions

Sometimes during a role-play, presentation, or conversation, someone might ask you a question that you don't know how to answer. One way to answer is to say, "I don't know." A better way to answer is to say, "That's a very interesting question. I'll have to get back to you on that." Then, research the answer on your own and share the information with the person who asked you the question.

# Health and Fitness

## Think and Discuss

1. Think of activities such as rock climbing that require extreme fitness. How do people prepare to do these activities?
2. What can you do to cheer yourself up when you feel sad or are facing a stressful situation?

Without a rope, a rock climber climbs up a wall in Yosemite National Park in the United States.

# Exploring the Theme:
## Health and Fitness

Look at the photos and read the captions. Then discuss the questions.

1. What is the steel room used for?
2. How can chemicals such as DDT affect your health?
3. Where is it possible to go rock climbing? What kinds of equipment would you need?
4. Have you ever tried yoga? What are the health benefits of practicing yoga regularly?

## Health Dangers

This steel room at Georgia Tech Research Institute is used to measure indoor air pollution that can affect our health. Small amounts of dangerous chemicals can be released from surprising sources including desks, electronics, and clothing.

A warning sign tells people to stay away from a building in Zambia where the government stores DDT. The chemical can be deadly if mishandled, but it can also be used to kill dangerous bugs.

## Rock Climbing

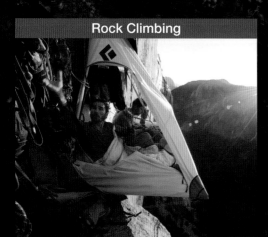

Rock climbing is more popular than ever before. These rock climbers stop on the side of a mountain as they take a break from their climbing.

A man is doing yoga on Wharaiki Beach in New Zealand.

🎧 track 3-10 **A** | **Meaning from Context.** Read and listen to the article about pesticides. Notice the words in blue. These are words you will hear and use in Lesson A.

Professor Steve McLaskey of the Maharishi University of Management carries organic vegetables from the university greenhouse to the cafeteria.

Before scientists discovered it was dangerous, DDT was used as a pesticide.

In the well-known song *Big Yellow Taxi*, the singer asks a farmer to "put away the DDT." DDT is a **pesticide**—a chemical compound[1] used to kill insects. Farmers throughout the world spray pesticides on their growing crops to keep bugs and other insects away. In the past, DDT was considered a safe pesticide. It was sprayed directly on children to kill insects and was even used to help make wallpaper for bedrooms. Since then, DDT has been **assessed** by scientists. After years of testing, scientists concluded that DDT was harmful to humans, birds, insects, and even some other kinds of animals. Farmers in many countries stopped using DDT after they learned it could be harmful. However, DDT was not **eliminated** from the environment. *small amount* According to scientists, DDT **persists** in the environment for many years. **Traces** of the pesticide have been found in soil, animals, and in humans all over the world.

In the past several decades, more and more markets have been offering shoppers the **option** of fruits and vegetables grown without pesticides or other chemicals. There is a growing number of people who **appreciate** these **organic** fruits and vegetables. People who buy organic food fear that the **constant** consumption of food grown with pesticides could be dangerous to their health. They worry that, little by little, small amounts of dangerous chemicals will **accumulate** in their bodies until the amount is large enough to cause health problems. Scientists are still researching the effects of pesticides on humans, but it is clear that the amount of organic food available is growing. According to the Research Institute of Organic Agriculture, people around the world spent over $50 billion on organic products and food in 2010.

[1]In chemistry, a **compound** is a substance that consists of two or more elements.

**B** | Write each word in blue from exercise **A** to complete each definition.

1. The word ___Constant___ describes an event that is always happening.
2. If a chemical ___persists___ in the environment, it continues to exist.
3. Foods and plants grown without the use of pesticides and harmful chemicals are ___organic___ foods.
4. When things ___are accumulated___, they collect or are gathered together over time.
5. If you have ___assessed___ something, you have considered it in order to make a judgment about it (for example, how good or how bad it is).
6. Chemicals that farms use to kill insects or to keep insects off of their crops are called ___pesticide___.
7. If you ___appreciate___ a person, you are grateful for the person because you recognize his or her good qualities.
8. ___Traces___ of a substance are very small amounts of it.
9. An ___option___ is a choice between two or more things.
10. When an item is ___eliminated___, it has been removed completely.

**A** | **Understanding Collocations.** *Collocations* are groups of two words that are often used together. Complete the collocations by matching each word from the box on the left with the correct word from the box on the right. Then use the collocations to complete the sentences. *(See page 208 of the Independent Student Handbook for more information on building your vocabulary.)*

| | | | |
|---|---|---|---|
| constant _____ | without _____ | evidence | a trace |
| show _____ | accumulate _____ | exposure | appreciation |

1. In the past, people complained that many natural sweeteners had a bitter taste. Today, however, manufacturers produce sweeteners _____ of bitterness.

2. J. Gordon Edwards believed that DDT wasn't a danger to human health. He pointed out that workers at Montrose Chemical Company in California wore no masks or goggles, but were never harmed by their _____ to DDT.

3. Scientists need decades to _____ enough _____ to declare that a new food is safe for humans to eat.

4. A gift basket of organic fruits is a nice way to _____ to your friends, family, or coworkers.

## Critical Thinking Focus: Asking Questions for Further Research

When you read or hear about a new topic, you may want more information or want to learn about another point of view. When you want to do further research on a topic, ask these questions.

> *What additional information would I like to know?*
> *What other sources might have information about this topic?*

Later, you can do research to answer your own questions.

 **B** | **Collaboration.** Read the information in exercise **A** on page 144. Then read the statements below. In your notebook, write questions for further research for each statement. Do research to answer your questions. Take notes and be sure to list the source where you found your information. Then form a group with two or three other students. Discuss your questions and research findings with your group.

1. DDT was once considered safe for humans.
2. DDT doesn't disappear quickly.
3. The amount of organic food available in markets is growing.

## Before Listening

 **Predicting Content.** With a partner, look at the photo and read the information. Then answer the questions.

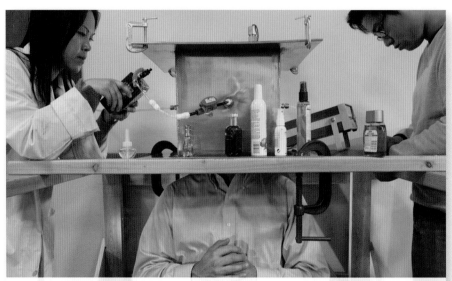

Household products such as detergents and perfumes can contain dangerous chemicals. Scientists test this man's reactions to different chemicals by spraying them into the box around his head.

1. How do you think chemicals in household products affect a person's health?
2. What dangers in food or the environment could affect a person's health?

## Listening: A Question-and-Answer Session

track 3-11 **A** | **Listening for Main Ideas.** Listen to the question-and-answer session that followed a lecture on health. Then choose the correct answers.

1. How dangerous are PBDEs to human health?
   a. Small amounts cause health problems mostly in children.
   b. Small amounts probably do not cause any serious health problems.
   c. Small amounts are linked to several serious diseases in adults.

2. How dangerous is lead paint to human health?
   a. It is a threat to the health of children.
   b. It is not a serious health risk for humans.
   c. It is mainly a problem for people who are sick.

3. How much swordfish and tuna does Dr. Wallace think is OK to eat?
   a. He recommends eating no swordfish or tuna at all.
   b. He recommends eating swordfish and tuna in moderation only.
   c. He recommends eating as much swordfish and tuna as you want.

4. Which statement is true about the danger of cell phone radiation?
   a. Cell phone radiation has caused cancer in people and rats.
   b. Cell phone radiation is not a threat to human health.
   c. Different studies have come to different conclusions about cell phone radiation.

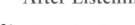

**B | Note-Taking.** Listen again. Complete the notes with information from the question-and-answer session.

PBDEs
 Impact on health: High amounts can cause cancer in _____
 Dr. W. suggests: For small amounts in humans, _____
Lead paint
 Impact on health: Small amounts of it can cause _____
 Dr. W. suggests: _____
Mercury
 Impact on health: Permanent damage to _____
 Dr. W. suggests: Eat fish _____
Cell phones
 Impact on health: Driving and using a cell phone can lead to _____
         Radiation from cell phones _____
 Dr. W. suggests: _____

## After Listening

**Discussion.** Form a group with two or three other students. Read the photo and caption below. Then discuss the questions.

1. If you had a chance to talk to Dr. Wallace, what health-related question would you ask him?
2. Would you like to be tested for chemicals? Explain. What types of chemicals do you think scientists would find?
3. What are some lifestyle changes you could make to allow fewer chemicals inside your body?

David Ewing Duncan had tests to find out what chemicals were in his body. He found out that he was carrying many compounds, including 16 types of pesticides. The compounds come from foods, drinks, and even frying pans.

## Language Function

### Expressing Uncertainty

Sometimes we want to talk about a particular topic, but we may not be certain that the information we have is correct. Here are some expressions to show listeners that we are not sure about what we are saying.

*It appears/seems to me (that) . . .*
*I'm not quite/altogether sure (that) . . .*
*It appears/looks/seems as though . . .*
*. . . appears/looks/seems (to be) . . .*
*I could be wrong, but it appears/doesn't appear (that) . . .*
*I'm not quite/altogether sure, but it appears/looks/seems (that) . . .*

track 3-12 **A** | In the question-and-answer session, Dr. Wallace used a number of expressions to talk about information he wasn't sure about. Listen and fill in the missing expressions.

1. In high amounts, they have caused health problems in laboratory animals. However, _____ the small amounts of PBDEs that normally accumulate in the human body aren't worth worrying about.

2. Large fish at the top of the food chain, such as tuna and swordfish, accumulate high amounts of mercury and pass it on to people who eat seafood. Now, _____ traces of mercury in the blood are a serious problem, but I could be wrong.

3. _____ you can eliminate radiation exposure from cell phones, but people who are concerned about it can reduce the risk by using a headset.

**B** | **Discussion.** Look at the photos. What is happening in each photo? Discuss what you see with a partner. Use expressions from the Language Function box above.

1.

> I'm not quite sure, but it appears that two women are helping an actress put on her makeup.

3.
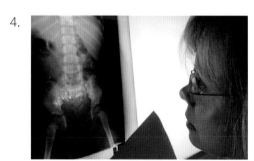

2.

4.

**C** | With your partner, read the captions that correspond to the four photos from exercise **B** on page 148. Write the number of the correct photo next to each caption. Did you and your partner correctly guess what was happening in each photo?

_____ a. In Mexico, a brick-maker faces exposure to the smoke from his kiln, an oven used for making bricks.

_____ b. A doctor looks at an X-ray showing lead paint inside the body of a two-year-old girl from Ohio. Even today, lead paint is still harming children who swallow it.

_____ c. People cover their mouths and faces to protect themselves from chemicals as they ride on motorbikes in Vietnam.

_____ d. At the Campaign for Safe Cosmetics in California, makeup artists exhibit chemical-free makeup.

# Grammar

## Phrasal Verbs

Phrasal verbs consist of two words: the first word is a verb, and the second is called a particle. (Particles are often prepositions.) Examples of phrasal verbs are *grow up*, *turn off*, *turn up*, and *throw out*.

phrasal verb

I **grew up** in the country, so I got plenty of fresh air and exercise.

verb  particle

*Some companies* **get around** *laws by illegally disposing of dangerous chemicals.*

Phrasal verbs are more common in spoken English than in written English. The meaning of a phrasal verb often has little or nothing to do with the words that make up the phrasal verb. For example, *blow up* means *explode*, *let down* means *disappoint*, and *put off* means *postpone*.

For some phrasal verbs, the particle can come after the object. For some phrasal verbs, the particle must come before the object.

*The solution to that problem is simple:* **turn** *your cell phone* **off** *while driving.*
*The solution to that problem is simple:* **turn off** *your cell phone while driving.*

👥 **A** | **Using a Dictionary.** Work with a partner. Read the book summary of *A Civil Action*. Use the correct phrasal verb from the box to replace each verb in parentheses. Use your dictionary to help you.

| | | | |
|---|---|---|---|
| finding out | got together | keeping back | thrown out |
| gave in | hold out | put back | turned down |

## Book Summary: *A Civil Action*

**Author: Johnathan Harr, Genre: Non-Fiction**

After (1) _____finding out_____ (discovering) that her child had leukemia,[1] Anne Anderson began to notice many other cases of leukemia near her home in Woburn, Massachusetts. It was surprising, because leukemia is a rare disease. Soon, Anne realized that something in the town might have caused the cancer. Eventually, she (2) _____ (gathered) with other families and hired a lawyer.

During a court case, a lawyer gives evidence to defend a certain point of view.

Lawyer Jan Schlichtmann (3) _____ (refused) the case at first, but later he accepted the case. Schlichtmann soon found evidence that the town's water had been contaminated by a chemical called trichloroethylene (TCE). Schlichtmann filed a lawsuit against the companies responsible: Unifirst, W.R. Grace & Co., and Beatrice Foods, Inc. The lawsuit was a long and expensive one, and he had to hire other lawyers to assist him.

Unifirst settled[2] for a little over a million dollars. The money was immediately (4) _____ (reinvested) into the cases against the other two companies. The case against Beatrice Foods was (5) _____ (dismissed) because of a lack of evidence. Schlichtmann found a former employee of W.R. Grace who knew that the company had dumped dangerous chemicals in the water. Though Schlichtmann wanted a high settlement, a difficult financial situation meant that he couldn't (6) _____ (wait) any longer. He accepted a settlement for $8 million from W.R. Grace.

Schlichtmann paid the money to the families, (7) _____ (withholding) expenses and fees. Some of the families thought that Schlichtmann charged too much, so he (8) _____ (yielded) and gave away more of the money. Schlichtmann would later lose his house and car and he even lived in his office for a time.

[1]**Leukemia** is a type of cancer that affects the blood.
[2]In law, **to settle** means to agree to end a lawsuit, usually for a payment.

👥 **B** | **Critical Thinking.** With your partner, discuss the questions.

1. Do you think that the result of the lawsuit was fair for the companies, the families, and the lawyers that were involved? Explain.
2. How could the city of Woburn prevent this situation from happening again in the future? Brainstorm some ideas.

## Discussing Environmental Health Concerns

👥 **A** | Work with a partner. How concerned is your partner about things in the environment that affect his or her health? Use the survey form to interview your partner. Check (✔) your partner's answer to each question.

| How concerned are you about . . . | Not at All Concerned | Somewhat Concerned | Very Concerned |
|---|---|---|---|
| chemicals used to grow food? | | | |
| chemical compounds in paints and materials around your home? | | | |
| chemicals in medicines? | | | |
| chemical compounds added to food such as preservatives,[1] colors, and flavors? | | | |
| chemicals such as mercury produced by industries? | | | |
| radiation from cell phones or X-ray machines? | | | |
| chemicals produced by plants and insects? | | | |

[1]**Preservatives** are chemicals that help keep food fresh for a long period of time.

👥 **B** | **Self-Reflection.** With your partner, discuss your answers to the survey. Give reasons for your answers, and give examples from your daily life.

> I'm concerned about chemicals used to grow food. I eat a lot of vegetables, and I'm not sure how they are grown.

👥 **C** | **Collaboration.** With your partner, think of three possible actions to take to protect yourselves from some of the environmental health concerns mentioned in the chart. Write your suggestions below. Then share your ideas with the class.

> We decided that buying organic foods would be good for our health.

**Actions:**

1. _____

2. _____

3. _____

---

**Student to Student: Going First**

Before making short presentations or talking with your group, use these phrases to ask the members of your group who will be the first to speak:

**In Pairs**
*Should I go first?*
*Do you want to go first?*

**In Groups**
*So, who wants to go first?*
*Will anyone/anybody volunteer to go first?*
*Does anyone/anybody want to go first?*

# Paraguay Shaman

Victoriano is a shaman in Cuyabeno, Ecuador.

Paraguay

## Before Viewing

**A | Prior Knowledge.** The video you are going to watch is about a scientific expedition to collect plants from a rainforest in Paraguay. Many medical scientists are studying rainforest plants. Form a group with two or three other students. Why do you think scientists are interested in studying these plants? Write down a few ideas.

1. _____

2. _____

**B | Using a Dictionary.** You will hear these words in the video. Match each word with its definition. Use your dictionary to help you.

1. potential (adj.) ____
2. renowned (n.) ____
3. extensive (adj.) ____
4. shaman (n.) ____
5. urgent (adj.) ____

a. a person who is believed to have spiritual powers
b. the ability to become useful in the future
c. needing immediate action
d. a large area
e. well-known

# While Viewing

**A** | Watch the video. Then circle the correct answers.

1. Why are the scientists interested in rainforest plants?
   a. The plants could help cure some diseases.
   b. Many of them are dangerous to eat.
   c. The plants could be a new source of food for the world.
2. What is Gervasio's part in the video?
   a. He wants to stop the scientists from collecting rainforest plants.
   b. He teaches the scientists how to survive in the rainforest.
   c. He leads the scientists to plants he knows about.
3. Why are the scientists in a hurry to find these plants?
   a. The plants are disappearing very quickly.
   b. There is little money available for collecting plants.
   c. Every scientist wants to be the first one to study an important new plant.

Deforestation is destroying many of the useful plants in the reserve.

**B** | **Viewing for Specific Details.** Read the statements. Then watch the video again. Circle **T** for *true* or **F** for *false*.

1. People in Paraguay are just beginning to understand that some plants can cure diseases.     **T**     **F**
2. The rainforest is disappearing more quickly in Paraguay than in most other countries.     **T**     **F**
3. Gervasio is looking for a leafy green plant.     **T**     **F**
4. Gervasio's wife uses the plant to prepare tea.     **T**     **F**
5. The book will help Gervasio learn more about plants.     **T**     **F**

# After Viewing

**Critical Thinking.** Form a group with two or three other students and discuss the questions.

1. How did Gervasio know which plants were useful and which ones were not?
2. Had Gervasio ever worked with scientists before? How do you know?

The Mbaracayú Forest Nature Reserve is home to thousands of different species of plants.

track 3-13  **A** | **Meaning from Context.** Read and listen to the information about yoga. Notice the words in blue. These are the words you will hear and use in Lesson B.

Swami Vivekananda

Yoga was **initially** practiced over 5000 years ago in India. In India, yoga is a tradition that is related to both religion and culture. **Prior to** the 19th century, yoga was not well understood and was rarely practiced in other parts of the world. The introduction of yoga to other countries is **attributed** to the Indian yoga master Swami Vivekananda, who toured Europe and the United States in the 1890s.

A woman does yoga on the railing of a bridge.

Many different **versions** of yoga are practiced, from traditional styles such as hatha and Sivananda yoga to modern versions such as chair yoga and laughter yoga. For fans of yoga, it is the **ultimate** workout because it involves not only the body but the mind as well. There are many health benefits associated with yoga. It helps you be more flexible, stronger, and it relieves stress. Yoga-style meditation[1] called yoga nidra can be very relaxing. Some yoga teachers claim that just a half an hour of yoga nidra is **equivalent** to two or three hours of sleep.

A yoga class in India

As yoga grows in popularity, more people are teaching yoga and more yoga schools and centers are opening. Since the 1960s the **expansion** of yoga has been remarkable, and today yoga is taught and practiced everywhere. It has become a truly **global** business with yoga retreats[2] in the United States, Mexico, Thailand, New Zealand, France, Egypt, and many other countries. According to **data** in the *Yoga Journal*, 14.3 million people in the United States alone practiced yoga in 2010. Scientists and researchers are now completing the first World Yoga Survey to count how many people around the world practice yoga. It is estimated that more than 30 million people practice yoga around the world and that there are over 70,000 yoga teachers. In many places, there are no laws controlling the quality of schools and teachers. Some people are asking for **legislation** to make sure the quality of yoga education remains high.

[1]In yoga, **meditation** is sitting quietly for a long time with a calm and clear mind.
[2]In a yoga **retreat**, groups of people go away for several days to practice yoga in a nice, peaceful place.

**B** | Write each word in blue from exercise **A** to complete each definition.

1. _____ is the act or process of becoming larger.

2. If B is the cause of A, then we can say that A is _____ to B.

3. The _____ form of something is the very best form of it.

4. Information, especially in the form of facts or numbers, is known as _____.

5. _____ means at the beginning of a process or situation.

6. If one thing is _____ to another, they are the same.

7. _____ of an item are forms of the item with some differences.

8. _____ means concerning or including the whole world.

9. If an event happens _____ a particular time, it happens before that time.

10. When a government passes _____, it makes a new law or laws.

**A** | Read the information and fill in each blank with the correct form of a word from the box.

| attribute | equivalent | initially | legislation | prior to |
|---|---|---|---|---|

A recent report stated that most illnesses can be (1) _____ to lifestyle-related causes such as stress at work or not being physically active. Joining a health club or gym can be a great way to get in shape and stay healthy. It's important to get as much information as you can about a health club (2) _____ joining one and starting to pay membership fees. Here are some things to do when you (3) _____ visit a health club:

- Take a tour of the club and inspect every part of it.
- Ask if members have to pay a fee if they cancel the membership. Some clubs charge members a high fee if they decide to leave.
- Ask about the qualifications of the instructors. All instructors should be certified in fitness instruction and life-saving skills or have (4) _____ qualifications.

It's also important to know your rights as a health club member. Most areas have laws protecting health club customers. Visit the government's consumer affairs Web site to find out about new (5) _____ about health clubs that has been passed.

**B** | **Using a Dictionary.** A *synonym* is a word or expression that means the same thing as another word or expression. Each word in the box is a synonym for a vocabulary word. Write each synonym in the box next to the correct vocabulary word.

| best | figures | international | maximum | overall | statistics |
|---|---|---|---|---|---|

1. data: _____, _____
2. global: _____, _____
3. ultimate: _____, _____

**C** | Use a synonym from exercise **B** to complete each sentence. *(See page 208 of the Independent Student Handbook for more information on building your vocabulary.)*

1. The World Health Organization is an _____ organization of 193 countries.
2. Going to college was the _____ decision I ever made.
3. I always set the exercise machine on the _____ level.
4. I added up these _____, and they are incorrect. Check your addition again.
5. The world has a lot of health issues, but _____, people are living longer.
6. The hospital input the _____ about your health history into the computer.

**D** | With a partner, discuss the questions.

1. Would you like to try yoga? If you have tried it, what version did you try?
2. What are the most important things for you in choosing a health club? What rules should health clubs enforce?

## Before Listening

 **Prior Knowledge.** With a partner, discuss the questions.

A rock climber uses a thin rope to cross over Yosemite Falls.

1. Would you like to try rock climbing? Why, or why not? If you have gone rock climbing before, describe your experience.
2. What are some of the dangers of rock climbing?
3. What kind of equipment do rock climbers use?

## Listening: A Conversation between Friends

 **A | Listening for Main Ideas.** Listen to the conversation about rock climbing.

track 3-14

1. What is the woman's attitude toward rock climbing?
   a. She wishes she had learned how to do it.
   b. She's concerned that it's dangerous.
   c. She thinks she'd be good at it.

2. Why did the man start rock climbing?
   a. For exercise
   b. For excitement
   c. To meet people

3. Which of these versions of rock climbing is the most difficult?
   a. Bouldering
   b. Traditional rock climbing
   c. Free solo climbing

4. Which statement about rock climbing accidents would the man agree with?
   a. Fewer people should go rock climbing.
   b. Taking some risks is part of rock climbing.
   c. Climbing should be done in climbing gyms.

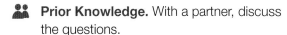 **B | Listening for Details.** Listen again. Match each version of rock climbing with the correct description below.

track 3-14

| a. indoor climbing | b. bouldering | c. traditional rock climbing | d. free solo climbing |

_____ 1. People climb on large rocks as high as 16 feet.

_____ 2. It takes place in climbing gyms.

_____ 3. People don't use ropes at all.

_____ 4. It requires lots of equipment.

**C** | Listen again. Then read the statements. Circle **T** for *true* or **F** for *false*.

1. A half an hour of jogging is equivalent to about an hour of rock climbing.        **T**      **F**
2. There are thousands of climbing gyms around the world.        **T**      **F**
3. There was a rock climbing accident in Yosemite last year.        **T**      **F**
4. Free solo climbing is no longer allowed in Yosemite.        **T**      **F**
5. There is one death in every 320,000 climbs.        **T**      **F**
6. Between 1990 and 2007, 40,000 people died in rock climbing accidents.        **T**      **F**
7. Stan tries to be very careful when he is climbing.        **T**      **F**
8. Stan has decided to give up rock climbing.        **T**      **F**

**D** | **Discussion.** Form a group with two or three other students and discuss the questions.

1. An *extreme sport* is a sport or activity that is exciting but dangerous. What other extreme sports are you familiar with? Do you participate in any extreme sports? What do you like about them?
2. Stan said, "If you don't take any risks, you'll never have any fun!" Do you agree with this statement? Explain.

## Pronunciation

> ### Dropped Syllables
>
> In some words, unstressed vowels sometimes can be omitted or dropped, especially in casual speech.
>
>
> every          mystery
> ev∅ry         myst∅ry

Listen to the words and cross out the dropped syllable in each word. Then practice saying the words with a partner.

1. int∅resting
2. vegetable
3. different
4. favorite
5. chocolate
6. aspirin
7. history
8. evening
9. generally
10. beverage
11. camera
12. restaurant

## Language Function

### Showing Understanding

In a conversation, you sometimes want to show the other person that you understand or sympathize with him or her. Here are some expressions to show that you understand someone's feelings or situation.

*You must be (tired).*

*That must be (fun).*

*You must have been (glad).*

*That must have been (difficult).*

 **A** | In the conversation, there were a number of useful expressions for showing understanding. Listen and fill in the missing expressions.

track 3-17

1. **Stan:** I spent today at Yosemite National Park. I was rock climbing.
   **Jennifer:** _____.

2. **Stan:** A half hour of rock climbing is equivalent to about an hour of jogging, and I was climbing for three hours today.
   **Jennifer:** _____.

3. **Stan:** The walls are pretty easy to climb—not too high—and the floor is usually pretty soft, so it doesn't hurt much if you do fall.
   **Jennifer:** _____, then, huh?

 **B** | **Role-Playing.** Form a group with three other students. Each person will take one of the roles below. Take turns role-playing each situation. Your group members will respond and use expressions for showing understanding when appropriate.

**Role #1:** You just got back from a two-week vacation in Europe. You visited London, Paris, Madrid, Rome, and many other major cities. You made some new friends, and you bought some wonderful gifts and souvenirs.

**Role #3:** You have an important job interview tomorrow. The company offers an excellent salary and benefits, including health insurance and a retirement plan. If you get the job, you have to move to another city.

**Role #2:** You just moved into an apartment that is brand new. It's in a really nice part of town, and the rent isn't too high. You have a lot of space, and the Internet connection is really fast.

**Role #4:** You are a photographer. You have your own photography studio, and you often take pictures of famous people. There is going to be an exhibition of your work at a local museum.

It's nice to be home. I just spent two weeks traveling around Europe.

You must be exhausted! What did you do there?

**C** | **Self-Reflection.** Work with a partner. Talk about events that are going on in your life right now. Use the expressions for showing understanding.

> I have two jobs right now.

> You must be really busy. What kind of work do you do?

# Grammar

## Three-Word Phrasal Verbs

Some phrasal verbs consist of three words. The last word of a three-word phrasal verb is a preposition. Examples of three-word phrasal verbs are *look forward to* and *get rid of*.
> I'm **looking forward to** going camping next weekend!

The object of a three-word phrasal verb follows the preposition.
> Are you going to **get rid of** your rock climbing equipment?

**A** | Work with a partner. Match each three-word phrasal verb with its meaning.

1. stand up for _____
2. pick up on _____
3. come up with _____
4. put up with _____
5. get down to _____
6. get rid of _____
7. come down with _____
8. drop in on _____

a. to endure or bear
b. to begin to suffer from (an illness)
c. to become aware of; perceive
d. to start doing something seriously or with effort
e. to visit
f. to speak or act in defense or support of
g. to throw away; dispose of
h. to produce or figure out

**B** | Use the correct form of each three-word phrasal verb from exercise **A** to complete the conversation. Then listen and check your answers. *(track 3-18)*

**Tonya:** Hi, Marc, how are you?

**Marc:** Tonya! What are you doing here? Isn't today your day off?

**Tonya:** I'm doing my grocery shopping and I wanted to (1) _____ you to say hello. Are you feeling OK? I thought maybe you had a headache.

**Marc:** Yes, I do. Maybe I'm (2) _____ a cold or something.

**Tonya:** Really? Why don't you just take some cold medicine? That usually (3) _____ my colds right away.

**Marc:** No, I can't. I'm working, remember?

**Tonya:** Well , why don't you ask if you can take the afternoon off? Just (4) _____ an excuse to tell the boss.

**Marc:** That's OK! I'm fine, really. I've got a lot to do and I have to (5) _____ work. Thanks for coming to check on me.

**Tonya:** No problem. See you later!

**C** | **Collaboration.** Write sentences using each of the three-word phrasal verbs from exercise **A**. Share your sentences with a partner.

## Sharing Advice

People often ask for advice on what to do in a situation. We use these expressions to share advice with others.

**Suggestions**
*You may/might want to . . .*
*You should . . .*
*You could . . .*

**Strong Advice**
*Always/Never . . .*
*Don't forget to . . .*
*Make sure (not) to . . .*

**A** | What advice about health and fitness can you share with your classmates? For each category in the chart, write two pieces of advice.

| Categories | Advice |
| --- | --- |
| Daily Health | 1. _____<br>2. _____ |
| Physical Fitness | 1. _____<br>2. _____ |
| Mental Health | 1. _____<br>2. _____ |
| Medicine | 1. _____<br>2. _____ |
| Food and Drink | 1. _____<br>2. _____ |

### Presentation Skills: Relating to Your Audience

Don't expect that your audience is automatically interested in what you have to say. It's important to grab the audience's attention. Here are some ways to relate to your audience.

- Tell them how what you are saying could affect them personally.
- Use words like *you*, *we*, *us*, and *our*.
- Encourage the audience to participate. Start some questions with "Raise your hands if you know . . ."
- Use real life stories to illustrate your points.

**B** | Work in groups of five. Divide up the categories among the members of your group. In the chart, circle the category you are responsible for.

**C** | **Discussion.** With your group, share and discuss each person's advice. Take notes on advice ideas for your category and prepare to present those ideas to the class.

**D** | **Presentation.** Take turns presenting advice ideas for each category to the class.

> You may want to brush your teeth after every meal, and don't forget to use dental floss.

# Mind and Memory

ACADEMIC PATHWAYS

Lesson A:  Listening to a TV Show
           Giving a Short Persuasive Speech
Lesson B:  Listening to a Conversation between Classmates
           Using Memory Skills to Recall Information

## Think and Discuss

1. How do animals show intelligence? Give examples.
2. What are some ways that humans show intelligence?
3. Do you think you have a good memory? Explain.

In Thailand, an elephant uses a paint brush and his trunk to paint a picture.

# Exploring the Theme: Mind and Memory

Look at the photos and read the captions. Then discuss the questions.

1. Which information on this page is most interesting to you? Explain.
2. What other animals may use tools?
3. How do humans use their memories? Give some examples.

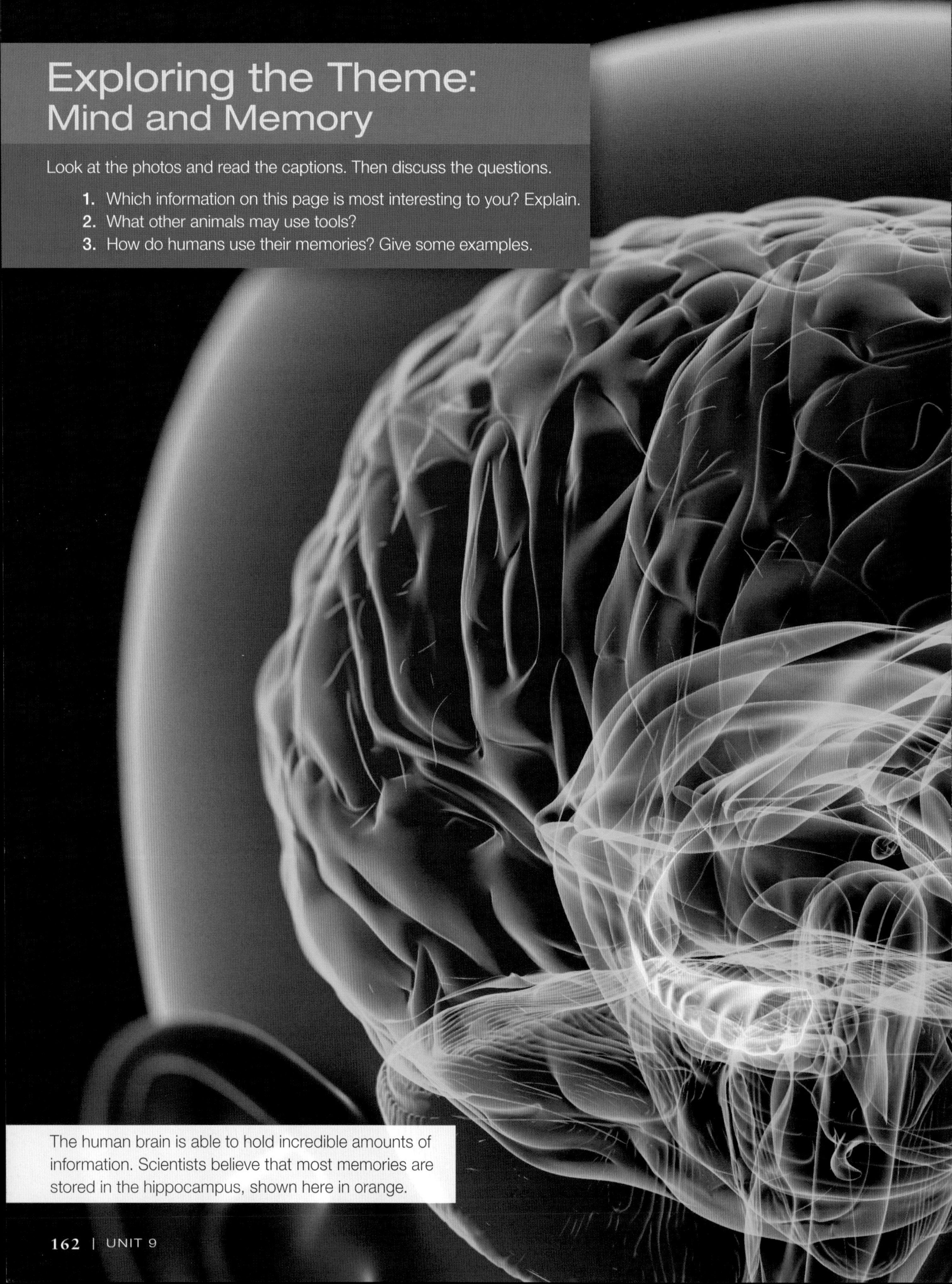

The human brain is able to hold incredible amounts of information. Scientists believe that most memories are stored in the hippocampus, shown here in orange.

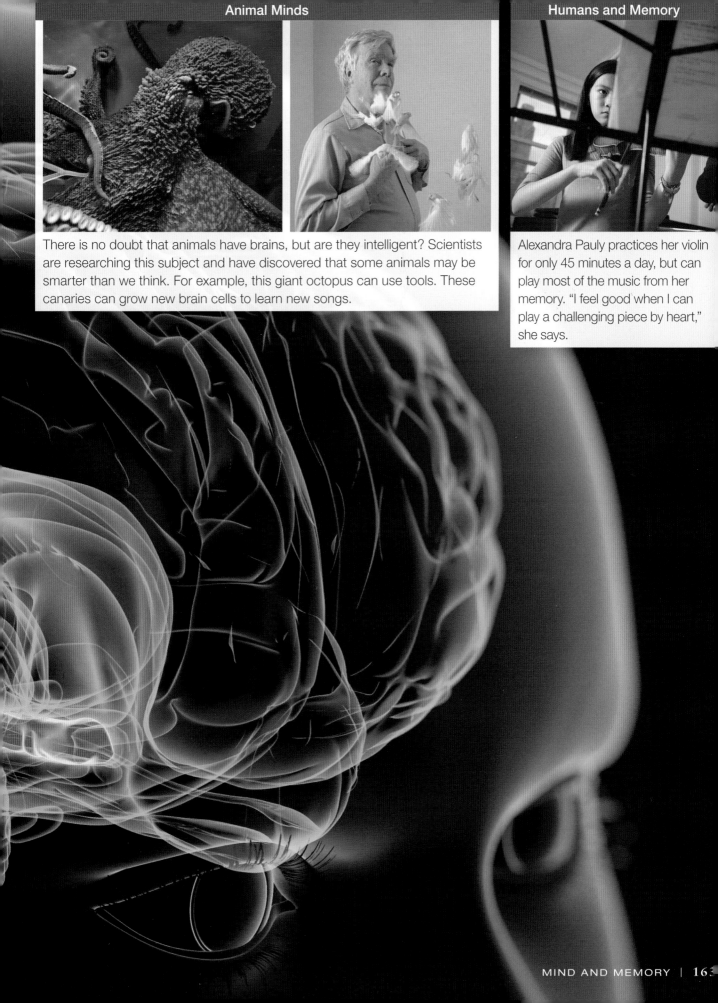

There is no doubt that animals have brains, but are they intelligent? Scientists are researching this subject and have discovered that some animals may be smarter than we think. For example, this giant octopus can use tools. These canaries can grow new brain cells to learn new songs.

Alexandra Pauly practices her violin for only 45 minutes a day, but can play most of the music from her memory. "I feel good when I can play a challenging piece by heart," she says.

**A** | **Using a Dictionary.** Work with a partner. Match each word with its definition. Use your dictionary to help you. These are words you will hear and use in Lesson A.

1. interpret (v.) ___j___
2. adjacent (adj.) ___c___
3. correspond (v.) ___h___
4. flexible (adj.) ___f___
5. illustrate (v.) ___a___
6. abstract (adj.) ___d___
7. motive (n.) ___i___
8. philosophies (n.) ___e___
9. capacity (n.) ___b___
10. underestimate (v.) ___g___

a. to show an example of an idea
b. the ability to do something
c. next to each other
d. based on general ideas rather than on real things
e. belief systems for explaining existence, knowledge, and thought
f. able to change easily
g. to think that something is smaller or less important than it really is
h. to have a close similarity or connection
i. a reason for a person's actions
j. to decide on the meaning of something when it is not very clear

**B** | Read the paragraphs and fill in each blank with the correct word from exercise **A**. Then listen and check your answers.
(track 3-19)

Are animals capable of showing concern for members of another species? According to the (1) _philosophies_ of many great thinkers such as Aristotle and Descartes, the answer is *no*. Recently, however, there has been a shift in the way many scientists think about this subject. The question is difficult because it is so (2) _abstract_. Let's look at one specific case.

A video filmed at a small pond in Africa shows an antelope trying to cross the pond. A crocodile grabbed the antelope and tried to pull it under the water. Just then, a hippo resting in an (3) _adjacent_ pond ran over and scared the crocodile away. The crocodile released the injured antelope. Then the hippo, trying to help, gently nuzzled[1] the antelope.

An antelope crossing a pond tries to escape the jaws of a crocodile.

How should we (4) _interpret_ the hippo's actions? It seems that the hippo's (5) _motive_ was to help the antelope, although the hippo didn't gain anything from it. The actions of the hippo (6) _correspond_ to what we in the human world would call altruism.[2] This video raises the question of whether we humans (7) _underestimate_ an animal's (8) _capacity_ to help other animals. This case can also (9) _illustrate_ how complex animal society can be. We should remain (10) _flexible_ and open to the possibility that animals can be altruistic, too.

[1]Animals **nuzzle** by touching each other gently with their noses.
[2]**Altruism** is concern for the happiness and safety of others instead of yourself.

**A** | Complete the paragraph with the correct form of each word from the box.

| abstract | capacity | correspond | illustrate | interpret | underestimate |

In the 19th century, Charles Darwin developed his theory of evolution. This theory claims that all living things evolved from other living things by small changes, little by little, over millions of years. If that theory is true, then it shouldn't be surprising to find that animals have the (1) _____capacity_____ for intelligence. In the first half of the 20th century, there was a shift away from Darwin's theory. Instead, *behaviorism* affected the way animals were seen. *Behaviorism* was a theory that ignored the possibility[1] of animals having intelligent minds. Today, many scientists agree that behaviorists (2) _____underestimate_____ the animal mind. Here are two examples of animals that (3) _____illustrate_____ intelligence:

Azy the orangutan communicates by touching (4) _____abstract_____ symbols on a computer screen. There are about 70 symbols that he uses. When Azy wants to say a certain word, he presses the (5) _____corresponding_____ symbol. Using this system, Azy is able to identify objects, ask questions, and even give commands.

Koko the gorilla is able to use American Sign Language to communicate. In sign language, you speak by making words with your hands. Dr. Penny Patterson, who takes care of Koko, (6) _____interprets_____ the signs that Koko makes with her hands. Dr. Patterson can communicate her own ideas to Koko using sign language as well.

Koko the gorilla uses American Sign Language to talk with Dr. Penny Patterson. Here, Koko is telling Dr. Patterson that she would like a pet cat.

[1] A **possibility** is a chance that something might happen or might be true.

**B** | **Discussion.** Form a group with two or three other students and discuss the questions.

1. What are some of the motives of people who work with and study animals? What do they hope to learn or gain from their work with animals?

2. A flexible mind is one that can easily adapt and make changes. Would you say that you are flexible? Explain.

3. What is your memory capacity? For example, how well are you able to remember names, dates, and telephone numbers after hearing them just one time?

## Before Listening

 **Predicting Content.** Work with a partner and answer the questions.

1. You are going to hear about the two animals in the photos. In what ways do you think these animals demonstrate their intelligence?
2. You are also going to hear about an intelligent animal that has a brain larger than a human's brain. What animal do you think it is?

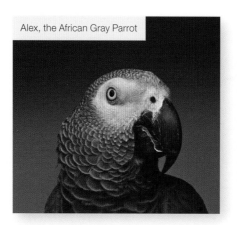

Alex, the African Gray Parrot

Betsy, the Border Collie

## Listening: A TV Show

track 3-20 **A** | **Listening for Main Ideas.** Listen to the TV show about intelligent animals. Choose the best answer to each question.

1. Which statement best describes recent ideas regarding animal intelligence?
   a. Scientists are comparing intelligent animals to machines.
   b. Scientists no longer want to study animal intelligence.
   c. Scientists are no longer underestimating animal intelligence.

2. According to Diane Willberg, how do parrots and crows demonstrate intelligence?
   a. Parrots speak, and crows understand abstract concepts.
   b. Crows can make tools, and parrots understand abstract concepts.
   c. Parrots can see colors, and crows can recognize tools.

3. According to Samantha Bean, how does her dog Betsy demonstrate intelligence?
   a. Betsy is able to recognize objects in pictures.
   b. Betsy is able to recognize herself in pictures.
   c. Betsy is able to recognize objects adjacent to their pictures.

4. According to Matthew Leonard, what animals have self-awareness?
   a. Humans, elephants, apes, dolphins
   b. Humans, apes, dolphins, dogs
   c. Humans, elephants, birds, dogs

**B | Note-Taking.** Listen again and complete the notes with information from the TV show.

Beliefs about animal intelligence:

- Descartes: Animals are _____

- Scientists today believe _____

- Ex. of mental skills of animals: Good memory, _____

  _____

Diane Willberg:

- Parrots: _____

  - Shows parrot 2 green objects. Parrot says _____

  - Shows parrot 2 balls. Parrot says _____

- Crows Lab experiment: D.W. puts a _____ in a bottle

  - The crow _____

Samantha Bean:

- In one room _____ In another room _____
  S.B. shows Betsy _____ Betsy _____

- S.B. believes this shows _____.

Matthew Leonard:

- Self-awareness is _____

- Exs. of self-awareness: humans, _____

## After Listening

### Critical Thinking Focus: Questioning Results

At times, you may hear information that you think is not believable or reliable. In these situations, you should question the results or conclusions of the speaker. Ask yourself these questions:

*Who completed this research? Could this person be biased?*
*Are the researcher's conclusions logical? Do the results make sense?*
*Did the experiment follow proper scientific procedure?*

**Critical Thinking.** Form a group with two or three other students. Discuss the questions.

1. Who do you think funds studies about animal intelligence? Do you think these studies are useful? Explain.
2. Do you believe that the animals described in the TV show are truly intelligent? Explain.

## Language Function

**Enumerating**

Listing reasons, facts, examples, or steps in a process is called *enumerating*. Here are some groups of expressions to help list information clearly.

To enumerate reasons and examples, use:
> *First, Second, Third*
> *For one thing, For another, And for another*
> *In the first place, In the second place, And in the third place*

To enumerate commands or steps in a process, use:
> *First, Next, After that*
> *First, Then, And then*
> *First, Second, Third*

track **3-21**   **A** | In the TV program, there were a number of expressions for enumerating. Listen and fill in the missing expressions.

1. **Diane:** Well, _____, I've found that crows are able to use tools and they can actually make the tools themselves. _____, my research shows that parrots understand abstract concepts such as shapes and colors.

2. **Samantha:** _____, I show Besty a picture, _____ she goes into the next room, chooses the corresponding object, _____ brings it back to me.

**B** | With a partner, look at the expressions for enumerating. Were the speakers in exercise **A** enumerating reasons, examples, commands, or steps in a process? Explain your answer.

**C** | **Collaboration.** Work with your partner. One student is Student A and the other is Student B. Read the statements. Write three reasons or examples to support your statement.

**Student A:** I am against using animals in circuses.
**Student B:** I am in support of using animals in circuses.

Reasons/Examples:

1. _____
2. _____
3. _____

**D | Discussion.** With your partner, discuss the ideas you wrote in exercise **C** on page 168. Use expressions for enumerating.

Animals shouldn't be used in circuses. For one thing, they're forced to travel on trains and trucks all the time.

A horse performs at a circus in Barcelona, Spain.

**E | Enumerating.** Work with your partner. One student is Student A and the other is Student B. Read the instructions about how to do one of the tasks below. Then, without reading, tell your partner how to do the task. Use the expressions for enumerating.

**Student A**

### Memorizing Information

You want to memorize the spelling of a difficult word or a long number such as a phone number. Repeat the word or number aloud. Break the word or number down into chunks or pieces. Put only two or three letters or numbers in each chunk. Repeat the chunks several times while looking at the word or number. After a few minutes, try to spell the whole word or repeat the whole number without looking at it.

**Student B**

### Changing a Flat Tire

Your car has a flat tire and you want to put a new tire on the car. Stop your car in a safe place. Use a wrench to loosen the lugnuts on the wheel. Use a car jack to lift the car off of the ground. Remove the lugnuts and pull the flat tire off of the car. Put the new tire on the car. Place the lugnuts back on the tire, but only tighten them a little. Lower the car back to the ground. Tighten all of the lugnuts on the new tire.

# Grammar

## Subject-Verb Agreement with Quantifiers

Quantifiers such as *none, a few, some, each, a lot, all, most,* and *every one* are used to talk about quantity. Quantifiers can be followed by plural count nouns or by non-count nouns: *some of the animals, some of the food*

When followed by a plural count noun, the quantifiers *all, a lot, some, a few, both,* and *most* take a plural verb.

> **All** of our dolphins **are** very intelligent.
> **Some** of the puppies **were** white.
> Chimpanzees are smaller than gorillas, but **both** (animals) **are** primates.

The quantifiers *one, none, each, neither,* and *every one,* on the other hand, are followed by a plural count noun and a singular verb.

> **Each** of my parrots **is** very special.

**A** | **Self-Reflection.** Complete each sentence with a quantifier. Make the sentences true for yourself. Try to use as many different quantifiers from the box above as you can. Then circle the correct verb form.

1. _____ of my parents (like / likes) to drink coffee.
2. _____ of my neighbors (has / have) a pet.
3. _____ of my classmates (think / thinks) animals are intelligent.
4. _____ of the scientists in the TV show (work / works) with animals.
5. _____ of my friends (own / owns) a car.
6. _____ of my co-workers (use / uses) a computer.

**B** | **Discussion.** Form a group with two or three other students. Talk about the sentences from exercise **A** with your group.

> Both of my parents like to drink coffee. What about your parents?

> Only one of my parents likes to drink coffee.

**C** | **Collaboration.** Work with your group. Talk about your likes and dislikes. Then write five new sentences with quantifiers about your group. Try to use as many different quantifiers from the box above as you can.

## Giving a Short Persuasive Speech

**A** | **Brainstorming.** Form a group with two or three other students. The chart below lists six roles that animals have in culture and society. Discuss these roles and fill in the chart with examples of animals that perform each role.

| Roles | Examples |
|---|---|
| Work | *dogs rescue people* |
| Entertainment | |
| Pets | |
| Research | |
| Food | |

**B** | Choose one of the roles from exercise **A**. Do you agree that animals should be used for this role? Write a sentence that shows your position. For example: *Animals should not be used for entertainment.* Share the sentence you wrote with your group.

**C** | **Presentation.** Now, each group member will give a two-minute persuasive speech to support his or her sentence. *(See page 211 of the Independent Student Handbook for more information on presentation skills.)* During your speech, you should:

1. State your position
2. Give examples and reasons to support your position
3. Restate your position in conclusion

**D** | After each member of your group has spoken, ask the group to vote on whether they agree or disagree with your position.

---

**Student to Student: Joining a Group**

If you need to join a group for a group work activity, you can say:

*Do you mind if I join your group?*
*Do you want to work together?*
*Do you need another person?*

---

**Presentation Skills: Using Gestures**

Even if you do not normally use your hands when you speak with friends, you should use hand gestures when you are giving a presentation. Gestures add emphasis to what you are saying and get your audience's attention. Practice your gestures in front of a mirror and make sure they look natural. Make sure to use various gestures, not just one over and over again.

# Animal Minds

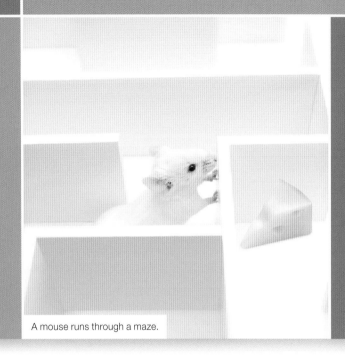

A mouse runs through a maze.

A dolphin looks at its reflection in a mirror.

## Before Viewing

**A** | **Using a Dictionary.** You will hear the words in blue in the video. Read the sentences. Then match each word with its definition below. Use your dictionary to help you.

1. Dreams show that our minds are working even **unconsciously**.
2. Don't use **coercion** to train an animal. Rather, reward good behavior.
3. Computers have large memories but no other **cognitive** abilities.
4. In 1859, Charles Darwin's theory of evolution came as a **revelation** to the world.
5. Whale songs are very **sophisticated** and could contain a lot of information.
6. I locked the dog in the room, but it **outsmarted** me by unlocking the door.
7. Seeing claw marks and brown fur, we **deduced** that a bear had gotten into our car.

a. _____ (n.) surprising knowledge that is made known to people

b. _____ (adv.) without being fully aware

c. _____ (v.) to reach a conclusion based on things that are true

d. _____ (v.) to gain an advantage by thinking effectively

e. _____ (adj.) relating to the mental process involved in knowing, learning, and understanding

f. _____ (n.) the act of forcing a person or animal to do something that they don't want to do

g. _____ (adj.) complex or advanced

**B | Predicting Content.** With a partner, look at the animals in the photos on pages 172 and 173. Scientists have found certain cognitive abilities in each animal. What cognitive abilities do you think these animals have shown? Discuss each animal with your partner.

## While Viewing

**A |** Watch the video. Then circle the correct answers.

1. What did a rat do that surprised scientists in the early 1900s?
   a. It followed a maze correctly from end to end and found the food.
   b. It got on top of a maze and used its memory to find the food.
   c. It completed a maze backwards as easily as it did forwards.

2. How do the trainers in the video shape dolphin behavior?
   a. They use coercion.
   b. They use a whistle and food.
   c. They use speaking and touching.

3. How did Karen Pryor cause dolphins to show creativity?
   a. By rewarding all behavior
   b. By rewarding only repeated behavior
   c. By rewarding only new behavior

A bird uses a stick as a tool to find food in a tree branch.

**B | Sequencing Events.** Watch the video again. Read the steps below. These are steps in the experiment Karen Pryor did to show creativity in dolphins. Number the steps in the correct order. The first step has been numbered for you.

_____ a. After two weeks, the dolphin had run through all the normal behaviors.
_____ b. The dolphin would start off with the behavior from the day before.
_____ c. The dolphin offered all kinds of new behaviors, for which the trainers gave the dolphin a bucket of fish.
_____ d. The dolphin and the trainers became very upset, and the trainers wondered if it was going to be the end of the experiment.
__1__ e. Karen picked a new behavior each day and rewarded the dolphin for it.
_____ f. In session 16, the dolphin offered a new flip followed by a new tail swipe, both of which were reinforced by the trainers.

## After Viewing

**Critical Thinking.** Form a group with two or three other students and discuss the questions.

1. Are you convinced by what you saw and heard that dolphins can use imagination and show creativity? Explain.
2. Do you think the rat in the video displayed more or less intelligence than the dolphin in Karen Pryor's experiment? Explain your answer.

**A** | **Meaning from Context.** Read and listen to the information about memory. Notice the words in blue. These are the words you will hear and use in Lesson B.

track 3-22

Memorizing the order of playing cards helps high school students in New York's South Bronx prepare for tougher academic challenges.

The amount of information that the human brain can hold is virtually limitless. Most people do not have an aptitude for remembering complex lists or numbers. Some people, however, use their memory much more than the average person. A person who is able to remember long lists of data such as names and numbers is called a *mnemonist*. This word is derived from the word *mnemonic*, which originated from an ancient Greek word meaning "of memory."

Each year, mnemonists participate in the World Memory Championships. This championship is a series of games that test a person's memory. Contestants are expected to behave in an ethical way at all times: there must be no cheating, no help from others, and no use of drugs that enhance the memory. Some of the events include memorizing numbers, words, faces, or images. There is also a "Speed Cards" event in which individuals must memorize the exact order of 54 cards as quickly as possible. The world record is 21.90 seconds.

One of the most successful mnemonists in the world is a British man named Dominic O'Brien. He has won the World Memory Championship an unprecedented eight times. O'Brien uses his own memorization method. He uses information he already knows as a framework, and adds new facts to this information. He says that practicing memorization techniques can result in a dramatic increase in almost everyone's memory.

**B** | Write each word in blue from exercise **A** to complete its definition below.

1. To _____enhance_____ means to improve in some way.
2. A person's _____aptitude_____ is a special ability to learn a task quickly and do it well.
3. A _____framework_____ is a structure that supports something else.
4. You can use _____virtually_____ to mean "very nearly."
5. If an event is _____unprecedented_____, it has never happened before.
6. A _____method_____ is a particular way of doing or completing a task.
7. If a word _____originated_____ from another word, it got its meaning from that word.
8. If something is _____exact_____, it means that every detail is correct.
9. A _____dramatic_____ change happens suddenly and is very noticeable and surprising.
10. An _____ethical_____ person is morally right or correct.

**A | Understanding Collocations.** The article below contains six collocations. Read the article and complete each collocation in blue using a vocabulary word from the box. *(See page 208 of the Independent Student Handbook for more information on building your vocabulary.)*

| dramatic | ethical | exact | method | unprecedented | virtually |
|----------|---------|-------|--------|---------------|-----------|

Who has a better memory: a chimpanzee (chimp) or a college student? The answer may surprise you. During a recent science experiment, Japanese researchers tested the short-term memory[1] of young chimpanzees against the short-term memory of college students. The (1) _dramatic_ result surprised everyone: the chimpanzees won. Many of the researchers believed that this result was (2) _virtually_ impossible, because the human mind is superior to the chimpanzee mind.

This chimp, named Ayumu, did the best on the memory test.

Chimpanzees beating humans in a memory test had never happened before—it was completely (3) _unprecedented_. "No one can imagine that chimpanzees—young chimpanzees at the age of five—have a better performance in a memory task than humans," said researcher Tetsuro Matsuzawa of Kyoto University.

The participants of the experiment were five-year-old chimpanzees and 12 college students. The chimps were taught the numbers 1 through 9 and their order. The testing (4) _method_ was as follows: Both humans and chimps saw nine numbers displayed on a computer screen. When they touched the first number, the other eight numbers turned into white squares. The test was to touch the squares in the order of the numbers that used to be there.

Japan

Often, neither humans nor chimps were able to remember the (5) _exact_ location of the numbers. However, to everyone's surprise, the results showed that the chimps could do the task faster. People who support animal rights feel that this type of experiment raises (6) _ethical_ questions. They do not believe that scientists should do research on the chimps at all.

[1]**Short-term memory** is information that we remember only for a short period of time.

**B | Discussion.** With a partner, discuss the questions.

1. The word *orangutan* **originated** from the Malay words *orang hutan*, which mean "man of the forest." Do you know where the word *gorilla* originated from? Suggest some ideas. Then research this information on the Internet to see if you were correct.

2. Imagine that you could take a medicine to **enhance** your brain in any way you wanted. Which part of your brain would you choose, and why? How would you use the extra power?

3. Do you have a great **aptitude** for a particular skill or talent such as mathematics or art? Explain.

## Before Listening

 **Self-Reflection.** Form a group with two or three other students and discuss the questions.

1. What are some of your earliest childhood memories? Do the memories seem clear to you or not?
2. When was the last time you had something to eat? What did you eat? What about the time before that? Continue and see how far back you can remember.
3. Do you have any tricks to help you remember things? What are they?

## Listening: A Conversation between Classmates

track 3-23 **A** | **Listening for Main Ideas.** Listen to two people talking about memory. Circle the correct answers.

1. What is "superior autobiographical memory"?
   a. It is the ability to remember many numbers exactly.
   b. It is the ability to remember details about one's life.
   c. It is the ability to remember new words and phrases.

2. What is the *hippocampus*?
   a. A part of the brain that controls memory
   b. A type of memory that cannot be lost
   c. An operation to remove part of the brain

3. How did Dr. Scoville's patient lose his memory?
   a. His brain was damaged in an accident.
   b. His brain was damaged by a disease.
   c. Dr. Scoville removed part of the patient's brain.

4. What is the location method?
   a. It is a way of remembering things.
   b. It is a method for operating on the brain.
   c. It is a way of living without a memory.

This artist helps solve crimes by drawing pictures of criminals. She bases her drawings on memories of people who saw the crime happen.

**B** | Listen again. Complete the notes with information from the conversation.

I. Superior Autobiographical Memory (SAM)

    A. Definition: _____

    B. How SAM works: _____

II. The Hippocampus (originated from words meaning _____)

    A. Dr. S Experiment: _____

    B. Result: _____

        1. Contribution to science: _____

III. Method of Loci/The Location Method

    A. Use: _____

    B. Steps

        1. Picture pathway that you know well

        2. _____

        3. Later, _____

## After Listening

 **Discussion.** With a partner, discuss the question.

Trying to help, Dr. Scoville permanently damaged his patient's memory. However, scientists learned a lot of information about the brain because of Dr. Scoville and his patient. Do you think Dr. Scoville's actions were ethical? Explain.

## Pronunciation

> **Using Word Stress to Clarify Information**
>
> To get more details from a speaker, listeners often ask a question by repeating what someone has said and adding another word for emphasis. The new word is stressed and said with a higher pitch.
>
> **Heather:** *So anyway, after he removed most of the hippocampus, he found that the patient had lost his memory.*
>
> **Maria:** *His **entire** memory?*

 Take turns saying these sentences to a partner. Your partner will ask you a question using the word in parentheses or his or her own idea. Be sure your partner uses word stress to clarify. Use your imagination to continue the conversations.

1. I bought a book of puzzles. (crossword)

2. I took an interesting test. (memory)

3. My mother bought me a car. (new)

4. He is a memory champion. (world)

# Language Function

## Checking Background Knowledge

Sometimes in a conversation, we need to ask how much our listener knows about a topic. Use these expressions to ask someone about their knowledge of a topic.

**Asking about familiarity with a topic:**
*Do you know (about) . . . ?*
*Have you (ever) heard of . . . ?*
*You know (about) . . . , right?*
*You know (about) . . . , don't you?*

**Asking for details about a topic:**
*What do you know about . . . ?*
*How much do you know about . . . ?*
*What can you tell me about . . . ?*

track 3-25  **A** | In Heather and Maria's conversation, there were a number of useful expressions for checking background knowledge. Listen to the sentences and fill in the missing expressions.

1. **Heather:** Well, we're having a memory contest in my psychology class.

   **Maria:** Why?

   **Heather:** Because we're learning about memory and the professor thought it would be a good experiment. _____ "superior autobiographical memory"?

2. **Maria:** Oh! I saw a TV show about that. _____ that show *Amazing Science,* _____?

3. **Heather:** Well, the scientists found that some parts of these people's brains are bigger than normal, including the part called the hippo—um, the *hippocampus.*

   **Maria:** I'm not sure I know what that is. _____ it?

4. **Maria:** I see. Memory is so important. I have a really bad memory. I'd love to learn how to improve it.

   **Heather:** Oh, there are lots of ways to enhance your ability to remember things. For example, _____ the method of loci?

**B** | **Checking Background Knowledge.** Work with a partner. Look at the list of topics that were introduced in Units 1 through 9. Choose two of these topics and find out if your partner is familiar with them. If so, ask for details about what he or she knows. Use expressions from the Language Function box.

Unit 1:  Tourism in Venice
Unit 2:  The Dusky Seaside Sparrow
Unit 3:  Eco-fashion
Unit 4:  Solar Power
Unit 5:  Wildebeest Migration

Unit 6:  Gross National Happiness
Unit 7:  Types of Payment Cards
Unit 8:  Types of Rock Climbing
Unit 9:  Superior Autobiographical Memory

> Have you ever heard of the dusky seaside sparrow?

> Yes, I have.

> What do you know about it?

> Well, it was a bird that is now extinct.

# Grammar

## Present Participle Phrases

Adverb clauses can sometimes be reduced to present participle phrases. These phrases show reason or time.

| | |
|---|---|
| **Reason clause** | ***Because** I have a poor memory myself, I'd be very interested in information on how to improve it.* |
| **Participial phrase** | ***Having a poor memory myself**, I'd be very interested in information on how to improve it.* |
| **Time clause** | ***While** he was trying to cure his patient, a doctor named William Scoville removed most of the patient's hippocampus.* |
| **Participial phrase** | ***Trying to cure his patient**, a doctor named William Scoville removed most of the patient's hippocampus.* |

*Sub-help* (handwritten)

Be careful that the subject of the main clause is the same as the implied subject of the present participle phrase:

**Incorrect:** *Jumping from the top of the bookshelf, **I** caught the cat safely in my arms.*
   (This means that I jumped from the top of the bookshelf.)

**Correct:** *Jumping from the top of the bookshelf, **the cat** landed safely in my arms.*
   (This means that the cat jumped from the top of the bookshelf.)

**A** | **Collaboration.** Match each sentence in the first column with a sentence in the second column. Compare your answers with a partner. In your notebooks, combine each pair of sentences into a new sentence using a present participle phrase.

1. He heard his master's whistle.  _b_
2. It recognized itself in the mirror.  _a_
3. It saw another bird.  _d_
4. It took the fish from the trainer's hand.  _c_
5. It uses a touch screen.  _e_
6. She lived with chimps.  _f_

a. The ape displayed self-awareness.
b. The Border collie turned to the right.
c. The dolphin made a happy noise.
d. The blue jay waited to hide its food.
e. The orangutan communicates with people.
f. Jane Goodall made many discoveries about chimp society.

Researcher Jane Goodall has studied chimps for nearly 50 years.

**B** | **Self-Reflection.** Complete each sentence below. Then change the sentence beginnings below to a present participle phrase and write a new sentence. Use your imagination. Share your sentences with your partner.

1. Because I am a responsible neighbor, . . .
2. While going to class (or work) each morning, . . .
3. When I see a puppy or a kitten in a pet shop window, . . .

> Being a responsible neighbor, I don't play loud music after 10 P.M.

You learned about the method of location, or the method of loci, in this unit. You can use this memory skill to help you prepare for presentations or remember information for school or work. To use the method, you put information along an imaginary pathway in your mind. When you wish to remember the information, you imagine yourself walking along the pathway.

**A** | Fill in the shopping list with items that you regularly buy at the supermarket or local stores. You will use the items in a test of memory.

**Shopping List**

| | | |
|---|---|---|
| 1. _____ | 4. _____ | 7. _____ |
| 2. _____ | 5. _____ | 8. _____ |
| 3. _____ | 6. _____ | 9. _____ |

**B** | Work with a partner. Look at your partner's list for 30 seconds. Then without looking at the list, try to say as many of the items in order as you can. Your partner will write down how many you got right.

Number correct: _____

**C** | Think of a path through a place you know very well, such as your home or neighborhood. Take about five minutes to think of images for each item on your partner's list. Place the images along the path in your mind. For example, if the path is your home and the first item on the list is eggs, imagine eggs smashed on your front door. The more creative the images, the better you will remember them.

**D** | Give the shopping list back to your partner. Then visualize your path and say as many of the items in order as you can. Record how many you got right.

Number correct: _____

**E** | **Critical Thinking.** Form a group with two or three other students and discuss the questions.

1. Look back at exercises **B** and **D**. Did your score improve after you used the location method? Do you think this method is effective for helping you to remember information?
2. How can you use the method of location to prepare for a presentation? How can you use it to help you study or take effective notes? How can you use the method to help you learn new vocabulary? With your group, brainstorm and write a list of ideas. Share your ideas with the class.

# Food Concerns

ACADEMIC PATHWAYS

Lesson A: Listening to a Powerpoint Lecture
Role-Playing a Debate
Lesson B: Listening to an Informal Conversation
Creating a PowerPoint Presentation

## Think and Discuss

1. Has eating food ever made you or someone you know sick?
What type of food caused the problem?

2. Who makes sure the food you eat is safe? How do you think
food safety could be improved?

Thousands of red peppers from Mongolia dry in the sun.

181

# Exploring the Theme:
## Food Concerns

Look at the photos and read the captions. Then discuss the questions.

1. How can scientists improve the way we grow plants and the way we raise animals for food?
2. What are some reasons for rising food prices around the globe?
3. Would you eat food that has been altered to include a medicine or a vitamin? Why, or why not?

### Our Changing Food Supply

Around the world, disease-resistant foods have improved the quality of life for many people. Some experts believe that genetically-modified foods could transform agriculture throughout the world.

Eric Anderson checks on the chickens at his farm in Arkansas. He uses antibiotics—drugs that kill bacteria— to keep his birds healthy. Consumers are worried that the use of antibiotics and chemicals in their food could cause health problems in the future.

Our Food Future

Workers shovel tons of soybeans on a ship in Victoria, Brazil. With food prices rising sharply, the world is struggling to feed its citizens. Scientists and governments are trying to find new ways to grow the world's food supply.

Student chefs prepare vegetables during a cooking class in China.

🎧 **A** | **Meaning from Context.** Read and listen to the information about the world's food
track **3-26** supply. Notice the words in blue. These are the words you will hear and use in Lesson A.

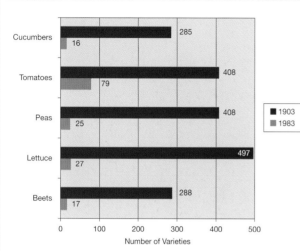

Cucumbers — 285 / 16
Tomatoes — 408 / 79
Peas — 408 / 25
Lettuce — 497 / 27
Beets — 288 / 17

■ 1903
■ 1983

Number of Varieties

A man holds two jars of peas at a seed bank in Norway.

The world population is now over seven billion
people. As a result, there is an intense need for additional
food. Instead of using conventional farming methods,
many large farms now only plant one crop such as corn,
wheat, or rice. Farmers plant this crop over very large
areas. This type of agriculture is known as *monoculture*.
The benefit of monoculture is to maximize the harvest,[1]
but there are experts who say that the benefit is offset by
its negative effects.

One serious problem of monoculture is the effect it has
had on the number of vegetable varieties grown by farmers.
The number of vegetable varieties has greatly diminished
since 1903, and many crop species no longer exist. In the future, if
one of the plants farmers rely on is destroyed via disease or climate
change, this could cause major problems in the world's food supply.
Therefore, some scientists are now trying to modify the genes of
other vegetables to recreate the lost vegetable varieties.

It's important to monitor and save the vegetable varieties that
remain. Many experts advocate setting up "seed banks" to collect
and keep the seeds of plants that are no longer planted by farmers.
Many farmers and scientists devote themselves to the important
work of setting up these seed banks. Today there are about 1400 of
them around the world. The vegetable seeds inside these seed banks
could be extremely important to the welfare of the people on earth.

[1]When farmers **harvest** food, they gather all of the food together.

**B** | Write each word in blue from exercise **A** next to its definition.

1. _____offset_____ (v.) to balance or compensate
2. _____devote_____ (v.) to spend your time or energy on a task
3. _____via_____ (prep.) with the help of another means or person
4. _____modify_____ (v.) to change something slightly, usually to improve it
5. _____advocate_____ (v.) to support a plan or action and recommend it publicly
6. _____welfare_____ (n.) the health, comfort, and happiness of a group or a person
7. _____conventional_____ (adj.) ordinary and traditional
8. _____intense_____ (adj.) very great or extreme in strength or degree
9. _____monitor_____ (v.) to watch or keep track of; to check regularly
10. _____diminished_____ (v.) became smaller in size, number, or importance

# USING VOCABULARY

**A** | Complete the sentences with the correct form of a word from the box.

| | | | | |
|---|---|---|---|---|
| advocate | devote | intense | monitor | via |
| conventional | diminish | modify | offset | welfare |

1. Scientists recently __modified__ the genes of an apple tree to grow bigger apples. They did this __via__ a technology called genetic modification.
2. The new type of apples are three times the size of __conventional__ ones.
3. The scientists don't __advocate__ selling the new type of apple tree yet because more tests need to be done.
4. The scientists have __devoted__ themselves to testing the apples for the next few months.
5. Representatives from agricultural companies are closely _very carefully_ __monitoring__ the tests.
6. Several food safety groups expressed __intense__ opposition to the trees, saying that they were dangerous. Scientists hope that the test results will __diminish__ these worries.
7. The agricultural companies and their scientists insisted that there was no danger, and that they always keep the __welfare__ of the public in mind.
8. The companies offered a large sum of money to __offset__ the costs of any health-related damage their new apple trees might cause.

---

### Critical Thinking Focus: Remaining Objective

When studying a new subject, particularly an emotional or controversial one, it's important to remain *objective*. Being objective means that you should be willing to listen to arguments on both sides of an issue. You should form an opinion based on facts, and should not let your emotions and personal feelings change your opinion about a topic.

**B** | **Brainstorming.** Form a group with two or three other students. On page 184 you read about *monoculture*. Make two lists: one with arguments in favor of monoculture and another with arguments against it. Then rank your arguments from most convincing to least convincing. Share your rankings and arguments with another group or with the class.

---

### Student to Student: Expressing Opinions

Here are some expressions you can use to express your opinion about a situation.

*In my opinion, . . .*   *(Personally,) I think . . .*
*If you ask me, . . .*   *As far as I'm concerned, . . .*
*As I see it, . . .*

## Before Listening

 **Brainstorming.** By genetically modifying plants and animals, scientists improve them for consumers. Brainstorm some ideas for improvements scientists could make to the plants and animals listed in the chart. Add two or three more of your own ideas to the chart.

|  | Ideas for Improvement |
|---|---|
| **Rice** | *They could create rice with vitamins in it.* |
| **Apples** |  |
| **Salmon** |  |
| **Cattle** |  |

## Listening: A PowerPoint Lecture

🎧 **A** | Listen to a PowerPoint lecture about genetically-modified (GM) foods. Choose the best
track 3-27 answer to each question.

1. In which order does the lecturer address these subjects? Number them 1 to 4.

    _____ a. possible negative effects of "gene flow"

    _____ b. a type of GM rice called "golden rice"

    _____ c. an explanation of GM animals and plants

    _____ d. where GM foods are being used

2. Which of these would be the best title for the lecture?
   a. GM Foods: The World Can Do Without Them
   b. GM Foods: Promising but Proceed with Caution
   c. GM Foods: Better and Safer than Conventional Foods

3. Which statement reflects the lecturer's opinion about the future of GM foods?
   a. More and more people will probably eat GM foods.
   b. They will remain illegal in most countries.
   c. Because they are too dangerous, few people will buy them.

These two Coho salmon are 18 months old, but one
was genetically modified to be larger than the other.

**B | Note-Taking.** Listen again and complete the notes for each slide.

GM animals and plants grow _____, _____, produce _____

    Exs. of GM experiments:

- Rat genes into lettuce to produce _____
- _____ genes into apple plants to help them resist diseases
- Modify salmon to make it grow _____ as fast
- GM cattle and sheep produce _____ in their milk

GM foods could be key to advances in _____

Critics think GM foods are being _____

    Exs. of critics' fears:

- Weeds with modified genes called _____
- Harmful effects on _____

U.S. has been eating GM foods since _____

    Exs: Pizza, _____, _____, _____, _____

    Countries with GM foods: _____, _____, _____, etc.

    Corps. offset risks through _____; Government monitors _____

Gene flow definition: _____

    Mixing GM plants with _____ plants could have long-term impact

    GM crops resist insects, insects could _____

- Result: _____
  _____

Golden Rice contains beta-carotene to help with _____ deficiency

Critics don't like that _____ control GM technology

Benefits of GM foods:

- _____ the amount of food produced
- offer crops that _____

## After Listening

**Critical Thinking.** With a partner, discuss the questions.

1. Do you think that the government should require companies to label foods that contain GM products? If so, what information should the labels have? Draw a sketch of what the label should look like.
2. In the lecture, the professor says that big companies control most GM foods. Why do you think some people are upset about this? What are some of the problems that could occur if only big companies control this technology?

## Language Function

**Confirming Understanding**

When you are giving a presentation, having a conversation, or explaining something, you need to make sure everyone understands the topic. Here are some expressions you can use to confirm that the audience understands the topic.

*OK so far?*                         *Have you got that?*
*Any questions?*                  *Are you following me?*
*Are you with me?*               *Does that make sense?*

**A** | In the lecture, there were a number of useful expressions for confirming understanding. Listen and fill in the missing expressions.

1. Many scientists feel that GM foods could be the key to the next advances in agriculture and health . . . _____?

2. In North America and Europe, the value and impact of GM foods has become the subject of intense debate . . . _____?

3. However, in the U.S. at least, food companies don't have to specially label their GM products, because government agencies haven't found any GM foods to be significantly different from conventional foods. . . _____?

In Shaanxi Province, China, farmers toss millet into the air. The wind separates the grains from their husks, or shell. These farmers still produce most of the world's food, but genetically modified foods could change that in the future.

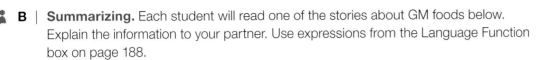

**B** | **Summarizing.** Each student will read one of the stories about GM foods below. Explain the information to your partner. Use expressions from the Language Function box on page 188.

**Student A** Edible Medicine

Scientists at the University of Agricultural Sciences in Bangalore, India, have created a new melon. The melon has been genetically modified to contain a rabies vaccine. Rabies vaccine is a medicine that can prevent the deadly rabies disease. Rabies kills thousands of people every year and infects many animals such as dogs. The genetically-modified melon is a cheap and easy way to provide the vaccine to millions of people. Additionally, a powder derived from the melon could be added to dog food to give dogs the vaccine. The fruit has successfully prevented rabies in mice. Scientists are now testing the fruit on dogs.

**Student B** Building a Better Tomato

Mark D'Ascenzo is a researcher at Boyce Thompson Institute for Plant Research in Ithaca, New York. He is showing a slide representing 20,000 tomato genes. Scientists are trying to identify the genes that make certain tomatoes resistant to diseases. "We've isolated hundreds of genes that are interesting candidates," D'Ascenzo says, "but we're still years away from understanding the whole picture." Once scientists do understand how to make tomatoes disease-resistant, the genes can be inserted into new tomato plants.

## Grammar

### Causative Verbs

Causative verbs show that one action causes another action to happen. Causative verbs can follow two patterns.

The first pattern is **causative verb + object + infinitive** (*without* to). This pattern is often used with the causative verbs *have, let, make,* and *help.*

   *The modified genes of GM salmon **make them grow** twice as fast.*

The second pattern is **causative verb + object + infinitive** (*with* to). Most causative verbs follow this pattern. Verbs that follow this pattern are *allow, assist, convince, encourage, force, hire, inspire, motivate, require,* and *permit.*

   *The government should **require companies to label** their GM products.*

**A** | Read the story about the use of GM corn in the Philippines. Underline the causative verb + object + infinitive structures.

## Philippine Farmers Adopt GM Corn

In 1991, the eruption of the volcano Mount Pinatubo ruined large areas of Philippine farmland. The hard soil and insect pests forced many farmers to give up on the land. Then in 2003, the Philippine government allowed farmers to plant GM corn. Although there were some fears about the dangers of GM corn, results of safety tests convinced the government to approve it.

A woman works on her farm on Samar Island in the eastern Philippines.

Global agriculture companies helped farmers get started and taught them to plant GM corn. Farmers used insect-resistant varieties that grow well in hard soil. Since then, the government has encouraged farmers to plant more crops. GM corn has enabled the farmers to produce more corn per acre (hectare) than ever before. In fact, GM corn has allowed farmers to produce three to four times as much corn per acre (hectare) as was possible before.

The success story of GM corn in the Philippines has motivated farmers to try other varieties of GM crops. Recently, Philippine farmers were winners of an international prize for outstanding agricultural projects. The prize is designed to inspire farmers to reach for excellence in agriculture.

**B** | **Discussion.** Work with a partner and read each situation. Use causative verbs to make suggestions.

1. The workers at a small restaurant are unhappy with their boss. The workers think that there aren't enough workers to help out during busy times. Also, the boss won't give the workers any time off.

> The boss should allow the workers to take a day off.

> That's a good suggestion. And maybe the boss should . . .

2. A grocery store owner is having trouble controlling teenagers who hang around the store. They seem to do whatever they want. They eat food in the store, drop it on the floor, and even steal some food. The teens don't seem like bad kids, but they don't have jobs or any other activities to do after school.

3. Some of my neighbors have been complaining about one of the houses in the neighborhood. The house is not kept clean. The windows are very dirty and the owner leaves garbage in the yard. The owner is a nice elderly man, but he's having trouble keeping up with everything he has to do.

# Role-Playing a Debate

You will role-play a debate about the positive and negative aspects of GM crops. Student A is an advocate for a concerned citizen's group and Student B is spokesperson of a GM company called GM Industries.

**A** | Work with a partner. Each student will prepare for the debate by reviewing the notes below. Add two more ideas to your notes.

---

### Student A: Leader of Citizen Group

- It's possible that GM crops could harm other insects or animals.
- Insects will get used to GM crops, and become difficult to control.
- Genes from GM plants can flow to other plant populations, creating "superweeds."
- Allergic reactions could occur.
- GM crop seed is expensive for farmers.
- Areas of some other countries have banned GM crops.

- _____
- _____

---

### Student B: GM Industries Spokesperson

- GM crops boost production. They are designed to harm pests, not other animals or insects.
- GM crops grow faster, are larger, and taste just as good as conventional crops.
- We need more scientific information on gene flow and "superweeds."
- GM crops are tested more thoroughly for safety than any other crops.
- With GM crops, farmers save money on fertilizer, pesticides, and farm equipment.
- Agricultural companies often work closely with local farmers to help farmers solve any problems that might arise around GM foods.

- _____
- _____

---

**B** | **Role-Playing.** Role play the debate with your partner. Try not to look at your meeting notes as you speak.

GM crops can be very useful. They are designed to harm only dangerous insects.

I'm not so sure about that. It's possible that GM foods could hurt other animals as well.

A farm in Greve, Chianti, Italy

## Before Viewing

**A** | **Prior Knowledge.** In Italy, the Chianti region in Tuscany is known for its beautiful landscape, wine, food, and for its pleasant way of life. What do you think people eat there? Discuss your ideas with a partner.

**B** | **Predicting Content.** The Chianti region is also the place where the Slow Food movement began. What do you think the Slow Food movement is? Share some ideas with your partner.

## While Viewing

**A** | Watch the video. Then circle the correct answers.

1. Which sentence best describes the little town of Greve?
   a. It is a traditional place with a comfortable way of life.
   b. It is an innovative place with a fast-paced way of life.
   c. It is a busy place with a hardworking way of life.

2. Which of these criteria would be important to someone following the Slow Food movement?
   a. The export of Italian culture to the rest of the world
   b. Appreciating what is special about each place and its foods
   c. Including more cheese and mushrooms in our diets

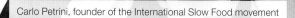

Carlo Petrini, founder of the International Slow Food movement

3. In what way did Salvatore Tescano follow the Slow Food movement?
   a. He ran an American-style restaurant in Florence.
   b. He closed his restaurant that served burgers and moved to Greve.
   c. He served more customers in Greve than he did in Florence.
4. How was the *Pecorino* cheese able to make a comeback?
   a. The cheese makers started using the milk of black sheep.
   b. The cheese was put on the menu at several famous restaurants.
   c. A campaign organized farmers and promoted the cheese.

Workers make *Pecorino* cheese.

**B** | Watch the video again. Complete the direct quotations from the video with the words you hear.

**Paulo Saturnini, Slow Cities co-founder:**

"Our (1) _____ and our duty is to try to maintain the soul, the essence, the
(2) _____ of Greve in Chianti, and all the other (3) _____."

**Sandro Checcuci, Greve resident:**

"It's very nice to (4) _____ because we have a (5) _____,
we have a nice landscape. And so when you have nice things to see, a nice place to live in,
it's (6) _____."

**Salvatore Toscano, Chef:**

"It means taking (7) _____, finding the rhythm that lets you live
(8) _____ in a lot of ways, starting of course, with what you eat."

**Luana Pagliai, Cheese Maker:**

"It's brought us a kind of fame. Not everyone knew about our (9) _____.
The project is getting us (10) _____."

**Luciano Bertini, Farmer:**

"From Singapore to Macao, in New York, and in Rome, you always find the
(11) _____, the same hamburgers. Slow Food doesn't want this. Slow Food
wants the specialness of every product to be (12) _____."

## After Viewing

Plates of figs and plums will be served to people at a Slow Food event in California, USA.

**Critical Thinking.** With a partner, discuss the questions.

1. In Lesson A, you learned about GM foods. What would a member of the Slow Food movement think about GM food products? Explain your answer.
2. What could the Slow Food movement do to gain more members? Brainstorm some ideas with your partner.

🎧 **Meaning from Context.** Read the definitions. Notice the words in blue. These are the words
track **3-29** you will hear and use in Lesson B. Then read the article below and fill in each blank with the
correct form of the vocabulary word. Listen and check your answers.

1. A **policy** is a plan or set of rules put in place by a government or organization.
2. If one event **coincides** with another, they happen at the same time.
3. An **apparent** situation or feeling is clearly true based on available evidence.
4. An **inclination** is a feeling that makes you want to act in a particular way.
5. If you **presume** that something is true, you believe it is true, although it may not be.
6. A **scenario** is a real or imagined series of possible events or occurrences.
7. The **scope** of a problem or issue tells you how far it reaches.
8. If you say that a situation is **the norm**, you mean that it is usual and expected.
9. **Output** is used to refer to the amount that is produced.
10. **Primarily** means for the most part, mainly, or chiefly.

Egyptians crowd a kiosk selling bread near the Great Pyramids at Giza.
Across the globe, there is rising demand for food but fewer supplies.

In the second half of the 20th century, there was a
dramatic increase in the amount of food farmers were
able to produce. Thanks to improved farming methods,
agricultural (1) _____ of corn, wheat,
and rice increased around 50 percent. It seemed
(2) _____ that scientists could
increase production of food as needed. People
(3) _____ that there would always be
enough food to meet the world's needs.

Today, it seems that scientists might have been wrong.
In recent years, shortages of important crops such as corn
and rice have become (4) _____, and with these grains in short supply,
their prices have been rising. The problem has been particularly serious for people who rely
(5) _____ on grain to fill their stomachs. The (6) _____
of the problem has been global, affecting consumers in Africa, Asia, Europe, and the Americas.
There is not just one explanation for these shortages, but rather several reasons that
(7) _____. One reason for the food shortage is that people are eating
more meat and dairy products. Both meat and dairy products require large amounts of grain to
produce. Another reason is the use of large quantities of grains to produce fuels instead of food.
Water shortages and the growing world population have also contributed to the food problems.

There are probably no easy solutions to these problems. It seems very difficult to ask people
to fight their natural (8) _____ to eat meat. A government
(9) _____ that makes eating meat illegal would likely be very unpopular.
However, some experts believe that we have no choice but to take action. If we don't, the future
may bring us unpleasant (10) _____ of too little food for the world's people.

**A** | Read the paragraph about the green revolution. Complete the paragraph with the correct form of a word from the box.

| | | | | |
|---|---|---|---|---|
| apparent | inclination | policy | primarily | scope |
| coincide | output | presume | scenario | the norm |

## The Green Revolution

The increase in agricultural (1) _____ of the late 1900s is sometimes referred to as the "Green Revolution." The increase was made possible when four farming technologies (2) _____. These technologies are:

- irrigation, a technology that brings water to crops;
- chemical pesticides to help kill or control insects;
- fertilizers, which give plants what they need to grow;
- and smaller plants that produce as much food as larger plants.

In India, workers pull loads of rice stalks to a farm to feed animals.

It would be a mistake, however, to (3) _____ that these methods will continue to deliver amazing agricultural growth. In fact, now that these four practices have become (4) _____ for farmers around the world, it has become (5) _____ that the increase in agricultural production can no longer be maintained. In fact, some experts have the (6) _____ to help start another "Green Revolution." They hope to avoid future (7) _____ such as food shortages, high food prices, and their consequences.

Scientists and government officials who determine agricultural (8) _____ are asking, what is the (9) _____ of the issue? These scientists are trying to figure out if there is any way to improve agriculture. To increase production, they are focusing (10) _____ on three different areas: the introduction of GM crops, the improvement of irrigation, and sustainable farming methods. Solving this problem could be the key to our future.

**B** | **Critical Thinking.** With a partner, discuss the questions.

1. A recent study concluded that science and technology in the past 30 years have failed to improve food access for many of the world's poor. Why do you think this is?
2. Thomas Robert Malthus, an 18th century British scholar, said, "The power of population is indefinitely greater than the power in the earth to produce subsistence[1] for man." Explain what this means in your own words. Do you agree with it?

[1]**Subsistence** is the condition of having enough food or money to stay alive.

## Before Listening

 **Understanding Visuals.** Look at the charts. Then answer the questions below. *(See page 216 of the Independent Student Handbook for more information on understanding visuals.)*

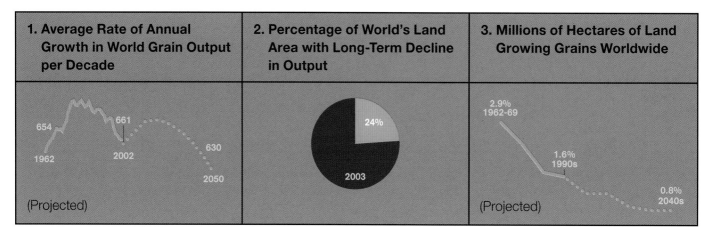

| 1. Average Rate of Annual Growth in World Grain Output per Decade | 2. Percentage of World's Land Area with Long-Term Decline in Output | 3. Millions of Hectares of Land Growing Grains Worldwide |
|---|---|---|
| 654 661 630 1962 2002 2050 (Projected) | 24% 2003 | 2.9% 1962-69 1.6% 1990s 0.8% 2040s (Projected) |

1. What will happen to the annual rate of world grain output in the 2040s?
2. On how much of the world's land was output declining in 2003?
3. How many hectares of land will be dedicated to growing grains in 2050?

## Listening: An Informal Conversation

🎧 **A | Listening for Main Ideas.** Listen to a conversation about food prices. Choose the best answer to each question.

track 3-30

1. Why don't farmers use more land to produce more food?
   a. They wish to keep prices high.
   b. The government restricted land use.
   c. There isn't any more land to farm.

2. What is the relationship between people eating more meat and the price of grain?
   a. As people eat more grain, meat prices fall.
   b. As people eat more meat, grain prices rise.
   c. As people eat more dairy, meat prices rise.

3. What have governments done to stop rising food prices?
   a. Stopped transporting corn from farm to market.
   b. Used corn in making fuel for cars and trucks.
   c. Placed restrictions on the export of corn.

4. What solution to food shortages do the experts suggest?
   a. They suggest increasing the output on farm land.
   b. They suggest finding more land to use for farming.
   c. They suggest government policies to stop eating meat.

**B | Note-Taking.** Listen again. Complete the notes with information from the conversation.

Problem:

    Rise in food prices over the past _____, quicker than the norm

    Most available land is already _____

Reasons for problem:

- Dev. countries have more _____ to spend, eat more _____
- Feeding farm animals requires _____
- Supply and Demand: If only a little food, but many want it: the price _____
- Some gov. policies restrict _____
- Some experts predict that areas of planet _____

Solutions to problem: Increase _____

- Increase output w/better _____ and fertilizer management; _____

## After Listening

**Critical Thinking.** With a partner, discuss the questions.

1. Which of the possible solutions to the global food crisis that you have learned about in this unit are the most appealing to you? Why do you think they might be effective?
2. Some scientists are predicting what they call a "perpetual food crisis" for the world. What do you think this means?

## Pronunciation

| **Syllable Stress** |
| --- |
| Putting stress on the correct syllable is important. Stressing the incorrect syllable could change the meaning of what you are saying. Look at the words below. When the first syllable of each word is stressed, the words are nouns. When the second syllable of each word is stressed, the words are verbs. For example, **pro**ject is a noun, while pro**ject** is a verb. |

| conduct | conflict | extract | project | reject |

**Collaboration.** Work with a partner. Write two sentences for each word in the pronunciation box. Use the word as a noun in one sentence, and as a verb in the other sentence. Then read the sentences to your partner. Your partner will monitor your syllable stress.

> Scientists will try to extract a special gene from tomatoes.

> I put vanilla extract into my chocolate chip cookies.

## Language Function

### Giving Recommendations

When discussing a problem, you sometimes want to give advice or a recommendation for how to solve the problem. Here are some expressions you can use to give a recommendation.

*Why don't you/they . . .?*                     *Have you thought about . . .?*
*If it were up to me . . .*                          *I think he/she/they ought to . . .*
*It might be wise (not) to . . .*               *It's (probably) a good idea (not) to . . .*
*If I were you I'd/I wouldn't . . .*

track **3-32**   **A** | In the conversation you heard, there were a number of useful expressions for giving a recommendation. Listen and fill in the missing expressions.

1. **Susan:** It seems that over the past five or ten years prices have been rising faster than the norm.

   **Andy:** Personally, I think _____.

2. **Susan:** When grain prices go up, they'll have very few other options.

   **Andy:** _____

3. **Susan:** You know, I heard that some climate experts are predicting a scenario in which large areas in Africa and Asia will become deserts. That might be a problem too, if the land is too dry to grow crops on.

   **Andy:** Wow. Well, _____, I'd try to get the whole world to work together to stop that from happening.

 **B** | **Discussion.** Read the statements. Form a group with two or three other students and discuss each statement. Use expressions from the Language Function box to make recommendations.

1. Although they are perfectly delicious and good to eat, many vegetables and fruits are not allowed to be sold in grocery stores because they are considered to be too ugly.
2. Fast-food is becoming more popular throughout the world.
3. Because of high prices they can get for their crops, some farmers are deciding to use land that was once reserved for animals for planting food instead.

An "ugly" carrot cannot be sold in grocery stores.

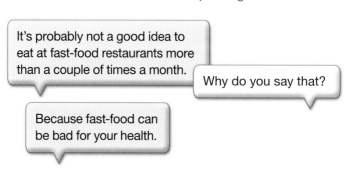

It's probably not a good idea to eat at fast-food restaurants more than a couple of times a month.

Why do you say that?

Because fast-food can be bad for your health.

# Grammar

## Subjunctive Verbs in *That* Clauses

The subjunctive verb is the base form of the verb (*be, go, have, bring,* etc.). The form of the verb does not change to agree with its subject.

> He recommended **that each country make** an effort to help agricultural output.
> They insisted **that their food sources be** protected.

Subjunctive verbs are used in *that* clauses (*that* can be omitted) following verbs of advice such as *advise, demand, insist, prefer, recommend, request,* and *suggest*. They are also used following certain expressions such as:

| | |
|---|---|
| *It is best (that) . . .* | *It is important (that) . . .* |
| *It is crucial (that) . . .* | *It is a good idea (that) . . .* |
| *It is vital (that) . . .* | *It is a bad idea (that) . . .* |

**A** | **Discussion.** Form a group with two or three other students. Read about these three people and their situations. Use subjunctive verbs in *that* clauses to make as many recommendations as you can.

---

1. A small island nation, which is a top exporter of pineapples, has been experiencing a terrible attack of insects. The pests have ruined the pineapple crop for this year, and there is no sign that the problem is going to go away. The president is looking everywhere for advice. What do you recommend that she do?

> It is important that the president eliminate the insects from the island.

2. Pierre loves to cook, and he does it very well. A few years ago, he even took a semester of cooking classes in Paris. Right now he works in a bookstore at a low-paying job, which he doesn't like. When he goes home every night he cooks a wonderful meal for himself. What career advice do you have to help Pierre?

3. Thomas is a young professional living in a big city. He recently got a job, and works six days a week. He usually eats toast in the morning, fast food for lunch, and frozen TV dinners. Imagine that you are a member of the Slow Food movement. What advice can you give to Thomas?

---

**B** | **Self-Reflection.** Think of two or three things that you need some advice about. Describe the situation to a partner. Then ask your partner to give you some advice. Your partner will use verbs and expressions followed by subjunctive verbs.

> I would like to learn to speak Spanish.

> It is vital that you practice every chance you get.

People from all parts of the world rely on the same types of foods: grains (such as wheat, corn, or rice), dairy products (such as milk, cheese, or yogurt), meat, fish, and fruits or vegetables. However, people from different places and cultures eat these foods in very different ways. You are going to prepare a poster or PowerPoint presentation about foods of one country.

**A** | Work with a partner. Choose a country whose food you know about or are interested in.

Country: _____

**B** | **Researching.** With your partner, research different types of crops that are common in the country you chose. Try to find a grain, a dairy product, a type of meat or fish, and a fruit or vegetable. Then find a food made with each item. Write a description of each food and an interesting fact about it. *(See page 211 of the Independent Student Handbook for more information on researching.)*

**C** | **Creating Visuals.** Create one slide for each type of food that you researched. Try to include a picture on each slide, if possible. Once you have created your presentation, practice it with your partner.

**Country:** Ethiopia

**Grain:** teff (an African grain)

**Name of Food:** injera

**Description:** Injera is a type of flatbread that is eaten every day by people in Ethiopia, Somalia, and Eritrea.

**Fact:** People tear off a piece of bread with their right hand. They then use the bread to eat a bit of stew or salad.

**D** | **Presentation.** Give your presentation to the class. When finished, ask the class if they have any questions, advice, or comments.

## Presentation Skills: Preparing Visuals for Display

When preparing visuals for a presentation, remember that they must be clear to everyone in the room. Keep people in the very back of the room in mind. When you are preparing your visual, ask:

*Is the size of the lettering large enough for everyone to see?*
*Is the language clear and easy to understand?*
*Will everyone be able to see any photos or graphics clearly?*

If necessary, make corrections to your presentation.

# Independent Student Handbook

## Overview

The *Independent Student Handbook* is a resource that you can use at different points and in different ways during this course. You may want to read the entire handbook at the beginning of the class as an introduction to the skills and strategies you will develop and practice throughout the book. Reading it at the beginning will provide you with another organizational framework for understanding the material.

Use the *Independent Student Handbook* throughout the course in the following ways:

**Additional instruction:** You can use the *Independent Student Handbook* to provide more instruction on a particular skill that you are practicing in the units. In addition to putting all the skills instruction in one place, the *Independent Student Handbook* includes additional suggestions and strategies. For example, if you find you're having difficulty following academic lectures, you can refer to the Improving Your Listening Skills section to review signal phrases that help you to understand the speaker's flow of ideas.

**Independent work:** You can use the *Independent Student Handbook* to help you when you are working on your own. For example, if you want to improve your vocabulary, you can follow some of the suggestions in the Building Your Vocabulary section.

**Source of specific tools:** A third way to use the handbook is as a source of specific tools such as outlines, graphic organizers, and checklists. For example, if you are preparing a presentation, you might want to use the Research Checklist as you research your topic. Then you might want to complete the Presentation Outline to organize your information. Finally, you might want to use the Presentation Checklist to help you prepare for your presentation.

# Formal Listening Skills

## Predicting

Speakers giving formal talks or lectures usually begin by introducing themselves and then introducing their topic. Listen carefully to the introduction of the topic and try to anticipate what you will hear.

*Strategies:*

- Use visual information including titles on the board, on slides, or in a PowerPoint presentation.
- Think about what you already know about the topic.
- Ask yourself questions that you think the speaker might answer.
- Listen for specific phrases.

### Identifying the Topic:

*Let's look at . . .*
*Today's topic is . . .*
*What I want to do today is . . .*
*Today, we're going to cover . . .*

## Understanding the Structure of the Presentation

An organized speaker will use certain expressions to alert you to the important information that will follow. Notice the signal words and phrases that tell you how the presentation is organized and the relationship between the main ideas.

*Introduction*

A good introduction includes a thesis statement, which identifies the topic and gives an idea of how the lecture or presentation will be organized.

### Introduction (Topic + Organization):

*I'd like to focus on . . .*             *To begin with . . .*
*There are basically two groups . . .*    *There are three reasons . . .*
*Several factors contribute to this . . .*  *There are five steps in this process . . .*

*Body*

In the body of the lecture, the speaker will usually expand upon the topic presented in the introduction. The speaker will use phrases that tell you the order of events or subtopics and their relationship to each other. For example, the speaker may discuss several examples or reasons.

### Following the Flow of Ideas in the Body:

*However, . . .*                    *As a result, . . .*
*For example, . . .*                *Let's move on to . . .*
*The first/next/final (point) is . . .*  *Another reason is . . .*

*Conclusion*

In a conclusion, the speaker often summarizes what has already been said and may discuss implications or suggest future developments. For example, if a speaker is talking about an environmental problem, he or she may end by suggesting what might happen if we don't solve the problem, or he or she might add his or her own opinion. Sometimes speakers ask a question in the conclusion to get the audience to think more about the topic.

### Restating/Concluding:

*In summary, . . .*　　　　　　　　*To sum up, . . .*
*As you can see, . . .*　　　　　　　*In conclusion, . . .*

## Listening for Main Ideas

It's important to distinguish between a speaker's main ideas and the supporting details. In school, a professor often will test a student's understanding of the main points more than of specific details. Often a speaker has one main idea just like a writer does, and several main points that support the main idea.

*Strategies:*

- Listen for a thesis statement at the end of the introduction.
- Listen for rhetorical questions, or questions that the speaker asks, and then answers. Often the answer is the thesis.
- Notice ideas that are repeated or rephrased.

### Repetition/Rephrasing:

*I'll say this again . . .*　　　　　　　*So again, let me repeat . . .*
*Let me put it another way . . .*　　　　*The most important thing to know is . . .*
*What you need to know is . . .*

## Listening for Details (Examples)

A speaker will often provide examples that support a main point. A good example can help you understand and remember the main point.

*Strategies:*

- Listen for specific phrases that introduce an example.
- Notice if an example comes after a generalization the speaker has given, or is leading into a generalization.
- If there are several examples, decide if they all support the same idea or are different aspects of the idea.

### Giving Examples:

*. . . such as . . .*　　　　　　　　　*. . . including . . .*
*The first example is . . .*　　　　　　*For instance, . . .*
*Here's an example of what I mean . . .*　　*Let me give you an example . . .*

## Listening for Details (Reasons)

Speakers often give reasons, or list causes and/or effects to support their ideas.

*Strategies:*

- Notice nouns that might signal causes/reasons (e.g., *factors, influences, causes, reasons*), or effects (e.g., *effects, results, outcomes, consequences*).
- Notice verbs that might signal causes/reasons (e.g., *contribute to, affect, influence, determine, produce, result in*) or effects (often these are passive, e.g., *is affected by*).
- Listen for specific phrases that introduce reasons/causes.

### Giving Reasons:

*This is because . . .*  *This is due to . . .*
*The first reason is . . .*  *In the first place . . .*

### Giving Effects or Results:

*As a result, . . .*  *Therefore, . . .*
*Consequently, . . .*  *One consequence is . . .*
*Another effect is . . .*

## Understanding Meaning from Context

Speakers may use words that are unfamiliar to you, or you may not understand exactly what they've said. In these situations, you can guess the meaning of a particular word or fill in the gaps of what you've understood by using the context or situation itself.

*Strategies:*

- Don't panic. You don't always understand every word of what a speaker says in your first language either.
- Use context clues to fill in the blanks. What did you understand just before or just after the missing part? What did the speaker probably say?
- Listen for words and phrases that signal a definition or explanation.

### Giving Definitions:

*Or . . .*  *In other words, . . .*
*. . . meaning that . . .*  *That is (to say), . . .*
*(By which) I mean . . .*  *To put it another way . . .*

## Recognizing a Speaker's Bias

Speakers often have an opinion about the topic they are discussing. It's important for you to understand if they are objective or subjective about the topic. Being subjective means having a bias or a strong feeling about something. Objective speakers do not express an opinion.

*Strategies:*

- Notice words such as adjectives, adverbs, and modals that the speaker uses (e.g., *ideal, horribly, should, shouldn't*).
- Listen to the speaker's voice. Does he or she sound excited, happy, or bored?
- When presenting another point of view on the topic, is that given much less time and attention by the speaker?
- Listen for words that signal opinions.


### Opinions:

*If you ask me, . . .*                    *In my opinion, . . .*
*(Personally,) I think . . .*             *As far as I'm concerned . . .*


## Making Inferences

Sometimes a speaker doesn't state something directly, but instead implies it. When you draw a conclusion about something that is not directly stated, you make an inference. For example, if the speaker says he or she grew up in Spain, you might infer that he or she speaks Spanish. When you make inferences, you may be very sure about your conclusions or you may be less sure. It's important to use information the speaker states directly to support your inferences.

*Strategies:*

- Note information that provides support for your inference. For example, you might note that the speaker lived in Spain.
- Note information that contradicts your inference. Which evidence is stronger—for or against your inference?
- If you're less than certain about your inference, use words to soften your language such as modals, adverbs, and quantifiers.


*She probably speaks Spanish, and she **may** also prefer Spanish food. **Many** people from Spain are familiar with bullfighting.*

## Summarizing or Condensing

When taking notes, you should write down only the most important ideas of the lecture. To take good notes quickly:

- Write only the key words.

  *dusky seaside sparrow extinct*

- You don't need complete sentences.

  ~~That's why the~~ Endangered Species Act, ~~which was~~ passed in the United States in 1973, protects ~~both~~ endangered animals and ~~their~~ habitats

- Use abbreviations (short forms) and symbols when possible.

  *info* information    *dr* doctor    *w/* with        < less than

  *ex.* examples    *b/c* because    = /→ leads to causes    > more than

## Outlining

Another way to take clear and organized notes is to use an outline. Like with other types of note-taking, in an outline you should only write key ideas and you should use abbreviations and symbols when possible. To indicate main ideas in an outline, use Roman numerals (I, II, III) and capital letters (A, B, C). Indicate details with numbers. As information becomes more specific, move it to the right.

    I. Background

        A. 1970s & 1980s: Soviet Union developed nuclear technology

        B. 1986: 25 plants w/ safety probs.

    II. Chernobyl disaster

        A. Causes

            1. Mistakes during safety test

            2. No containment building to limit fire and radiation

        B. Result: explosion → people dead

## Recognizing Organization

When you listen to a speaker, you practice the skill of noticing that speaker's organization. As you get in the habit of recognizing the organizational structure, you can use it to structure your notes in a similar way. Review the signal words and phrases from the Improving Your Listening Skills section in this handbook.

Some basic organizational structures are:

- Narrative (often used in history or literature)
- Process (almost any field, but especially in the sciences)
- Cause and Effect (history, psychology, sociology)
- Classification (any field, including art, music, literature, sciences, history)
- Problem and Solution

## Using Graphic Organizers

Graphic organizers can be very useful tools if you want to rewrite your notes. Once you've identified the speaker's organizational structure, you can choose the best graphic organizer to show the ideas. See the Resources section on page 214 in this handbook for more information.

## Distinguishing between Relevant and Irrelevant Information

Remember that not everything a speaker says is noteworthy. A lecturer or presenter will usually signal important information you should take notes on.

### Signals for Important Information:

*Don't forget that . . .*
*It is important to note/remember that . . .*

*Let me stress that . . .*
*You need to remember that . . .*

Instructors and other lecturers may also signal when to stop taking notes.

### Signals to Stop Taking Notes:

*You can find this in your handout . . .*
*You don't have to write all this down . . .*

*This won't be on your test . . .*
*This information is in your book . . .*

In a similar way, they may let you know when they are going to discuss something off-topic.

### Understanding Sidetracks:

*That reminds me . . .*
*On a different topic . . .*
*This is off the subject, but . . .*

*Incidentally . . .*
*As an aside . . .*
*By the way, . . .*

## Recognizing a Return to a Previous Topic

When a speaker makes a sidetrack and talks about something that is not directly related to the main topic, he or she will often signal a return to a previous topic.

### Returning to a Previous Topic:

*Back to . . .*
*To continue . . .*
*So, just to restate . . .*
*OK, so to get back on topic . . .*
*Getting back to what we were saying . . .*
*To return to what we were talking about earlier . . .*

## Using Notes Effectively

It's important to not only take good notes, but also to use them in the most effective way.

*Strategies:*

- Go over your notes after class to review and add information you might have forgotten to write down.
- Compare notes with a classmate or study group to make sure you have all the important information.
- Review your notes before the next class, so you will understand and remember the information better.

## Independent Vocabulary Learning Tips

**Keep a vocabulary journal.**

- If a new word is useful, write it in a special notebook. Also write a short definition (in English if possible) and the sentence or situation where you found the word (its context). Write your own sentence that uses the word.
- Carry your vocabulary notebook with you at all times. Review the words whenever you have free time.
- Choose vocabulary words that will be useful to you. Some words are rarely used.

**Experiment with new vocabulary.**

- Think about new vocabulary in different ways. For example, look at all the words in your vocabulary journal and make a list of only the verbs. Or, list the words according to the number of syllables (one-syllable words, two-syllable words, and so on).
- Use new vocabulary to write a poem, a story, or an email message to a friend.
- Use an online dictionary to listen to the sound of new words. If possible, make a list of words that rhyme. Brainstorm words that relate to a single topic that begin with the same sound (*student, study, school, skills, strategies, studious*).

**Use new words as often as possible.**

- You will not know a new vocabulary word after hearing or reading it once. You need to remember the word several times before it enters your long-term memory.
- The way you use an English word—in which situations and with what other words—might be different from a similar word in your first language. If you use your new vocabulary often, you're more likely to discover the correct way to use it.

**Use vocabulary organizers.**

- Label pictures.

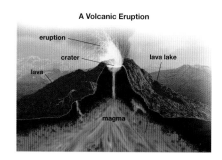

- Make word maps.

- Make personal flashcards. Write the words you want to learn on one side. Write the definition and/or an example sentence on the other.

# Prefixes and Suffixes

Use prefixes and suffixes to guess the meaning of unfamiliar words and to expand your vocabulary. Prefixes usually change the meaning of a word somewhat. Suffixes usually change the part of speech. If you train yourself to look for the base meaning, or the meaning of the stem of the word, you can understand more vocabulary.

| Prefix | Meaning | Example |
|--------|---------|---------|
| a- | completely; not | awake; apolitical |
| bi- | two | bilingual, bicycle |
| dis- | not, negation, removal | disappear, disadvantages |
| pre- | before | prehistoric, preheat |
| mis- | bad, badly, incorrectly | misunderstand, misjudge |
| re- | again | remove |
| un- | not, the opposite of | unhappy, unusual, unbelievable |

The following are derivational suffixes that change the part of speech of the base word.

| Suffix | New Part of Speech | Example |
|--------|--------------------|---------|
| -able | adjective | believable |
| -ary | noun | summary |
| -ent | adjective | convergent, divergent |
| -ful | adjective | beautiful, successful |
| -ed | adjective | stressed, interested |
| -ize | verb | summarize |
| -ly | adverb | carefully, completely |
| -ment | noun | assignment |
| -tion | noun | information |

# Dictionary Skills

The dictionary listing for a word usually provides the pronunciation, part of speech, other word forms, synonyms, examples of sentences that show the word in context, and common collocations.

## Synonyms
A *synonym* is a word that means the same thing (e.g., *baby=infant*). Use synonyms to expand your vocabulary.

## Word Families
These are the words that have the same stem or base word, but have different prefixes or suffixes.

## Different Meanings of the Same Word
Many words have several meanings and several parts of speech. The example sentences in the word's dictionary entry can help you determine which meaning you need. For example, the word *plant* can be a noun or a verb.

## Collocations
Dictionary entries often provide *collocations*, or words that are often used with the target word. For example, if you look up the word *get*, you might see *get around*, *get into*, *get there*, and so on.

## Everyday Communication

### Summary of Useful Phrases for Everyday Communication

It's important to practice speaking English every day, with your teacher, your classmates, and anyone else you can find to practice with. This chart lists common phrases you can use in everyday communication situations. The phrases are listed in this chart from more formal to less formal.

| | |
|---|---|
| **Asking for Clarification:**<br>*Could you explain . . . (for me, please)?*<br>*What do you mean by . . . ?*<br>*What (exactly) is . . . ?*<br>*(Sorry,) what does . . . mean?* | **Digressing from the Topic:**<br>*Speaking of . . .*<br>*That reminds me, . . .*<br>*Incidentally . . .*<br>*By the way . . .* |
| **Agreeing:**<br>*I agree.*<br>*I think so too.*<br>*I think you're right.*<br>*Exactly!*<br>*You can say that again!* | **Expressing Hopes:**<br>*It would be nice/great/wonderful/ideal if . . .*<br>*I'm hoping (that) . . .*<br>*I (really) hope (that) . . .* |
| **Disagreeing:**<br>*I disagree.*<br>*I'm not so sure (about that) . . .*<br>*That's debatable.*<br>*I don't think so.*<br>*That's crazy!*<br>*No way!* | **Apologizing for Interrupting:**<br>*I'm sorry. I didn't mean to cut you off.*<br>*What were you going to say?*<br>*Go ahead.*<br>*Sorry.* |
| **Conceding a Point:**<br>*Good point.*<br>*Fair enough.*<br>*I'll give you that.* | **Asking Sensitive Questions:**<br>*Excuse me for asking, but . . . ?*<br>*Do you mind if I ask you . . . ?*<br>*If you don't mind my asking, . . .?* |
| **Expressing Surprise:**<br>*That's amazing/astonishing/incredible.*<br>*That's (really) surprising.*<br>*Wow!*<br>*No kidding.*<br>*Imagine that!* | **Congratulating the Group:**<br>*Nice job, everybody!*<br>*Congratulations!*<br>*We make a great team!*<br>*Great going, gang!*<br>*Good for you!*<br>*Way to go, guys!* |
| **Expressing Encouragement:**<br>*Good luck!*<br>*Go for it!*<br>*Go get 'em!* | **Expressing Interest:**<br>*Is that so?*<br>*How interesting!*<br>*I didn't know that.* |

| | |
|---|---|
| **Expressing Approval and Disapproval:**<br>*(I) think it's fine to . . .*<br>*It's OK that . . .*<br>*It's not right for (someone) to . . .*<br>*It's wrong to . . .* | **Joining a Group:**<br>*Do you mind if I join your group?*<br>*Do you want to work together?*<br>*Do you need another person?* |
| **Enumerating:**<br>*First, . . . Second, . . . Third, . . .*<br>*First . . . , then . . . , and then . . .*<br>*For one thing, . . . For another, . . .*<br>   *And for another, . . .* | **Checking Background Knowledge:**<br>*Do you know about . . . ?*<br>*Have you (ever) heard of . . . ?*<br>*What do you know about . . . ?*<br>*What can you tell me about . . . ?* |

## Doing Group Projects

You will often have to work with a group on activities and projects. It can be helpful to assign group members certain roles. You should try to switch roles every time you do a new activity. Here is a description of some common roles used in group activities and projects:

***Group Leader***—Makes sure the assignment is done correctly and all group members participate. Asks questions: *What do you think? Does anyone have another idea?*

***Secretary***—Takes notes on the group's ideas (including a plan for sharing the work).

***Manager***—During the planning and practice phases, the manager makes sure the presentation can be given within the time limit. If possible, practice the presentation from beginning to end and time it.

***Expert***—Understands the topic well; invites and answers audience questions after the presentation. Make a list of possible questions ahead of time to be prepared.

***Coach***—Reminds group members to perform their assigned roles in the group work.

Note that group members have one of these roles in addition to their contribution to the presentation content and delivery.

## Classroom Presentation Skills

### Library Research

If you can go to a public library or school library, start there. You don't have to read whole books. Parts of books, magazines, newspapers, and even videos are all possible sources of information. A librarian can help you find both print and online sources of information.

## Online Research

The Internet is a source with a lot of information, but it has to be looked at carefully. Many Web sites are commercial and may have incomplete, inaccurate, or biased information.

### Finding reliable sources

*Strategies:*

- Your sources of information need to be reliable. Think about the author and the publisher. Ask yourself: *What is their point of view? Can I trust this information?*
- Your sources need to be well respected. For example, an article from *The Lancet* (a journal of medical news) will probably be more respected than an article from a popular magazine.
- Start with Web sites with *.edu* or *.org* endings. These are usually educational or non-commercial Web sites. Some *.com* Web sites also have good information, for example www.nationalgeographic.com or www.britannica.com.

### Finding information that is appropriate for your topic

*Strategies:*

- Look for up-to-date information, especially in fields that change often such as technology or business. For Internet sources, look for recent updates to the Web sites.
- Most of the time, you'll need to find more than one source of information. Find sources that are long enough to contain some good information, but not so long that you won't have time to read them.
- Think about the source's audience. For example, imagine that you are buying a new computer and want to read about the different types of computers before you buy one. If the source is written for computer programmers, for example, you might not be able to understand it. If the source is written for university students who need to buy a new computer, it's more likely to be understandable.

## Speaking Clearly and Comprehensibly

It's important that your audience understands what you are saying for your presentation to be effective.

*Strategies:*

- Practice your presentation many times for at least one other person and ask him or her for feedback.
- Make sure you know the correct pronunciation of every word—especially the ones you will say more than once. Look them up online or ask your instructor for the correct pronunciation.
- Try to use thought groups. Keep these words together: long subjects, verbs and objects, clauses, prepositional phrases. Remember to pause slightly at all punctuation and between thought groups.
- Speak loudly enough so that everyone can hear.
- Stop occasionally to ask your audience if they can hear you and follow what you are saying.

## Demonstrating Knowledge of Content

You should know more about your subject than you actually say in your presentation. Your audience may have questions or you may need to explain something in more detail than you planned. Knowing a lot about your subject will allow you to present well and feel more confident.

*Strategies:*

- Practice your presentation several times.
- Don't read your notes.
- Say more than is on your visuals.
- Tell your audience what the visuals mean.

### Phrases to Talk about Visuals:

*You can see . . .*
*The main point is that . . .*
*The line/box represents . . .*
*This graph/diagram shows/explains . . .*

## Engaging the Audience

Presenting is an important skill. If your audience isn't interested in what you have to say, then your message is lost.

*Strategies:*

- Introduce yourself.
- Make eye contact. Look around at different people in the audience.
- Use good posture. *Posture* means how you hold your body. When you speak in front of the class, you should stand up straight. Hold your hands together in front of your waist, if you aren't holding notes. This shows that you are confident and well prepared.
- Pause to check understanding. When you present ideas, it's important to find out if your audience understands you. Look at the faces of people in the audience. Do they look confused? Use the expressions from the chart below to check understanding.

### Phrases to Check for Understanding:

*OK so far?*
*Are you with me?*
*Have you got that?*
*Does that make sense?*
*Do you have any questions?*

# Understanding and Using Visuals: Graphic Organizers

## T-Chart

**Purpose:** Compare or contrast two things or list aspects of two things

| GM Food: Pros | GM Food: Cons |
|---|---|
| pest-resistant crops | could be dangerous |

## Venn Diagram

**Purpose:** Show differences and similarities between two things, sometimes three

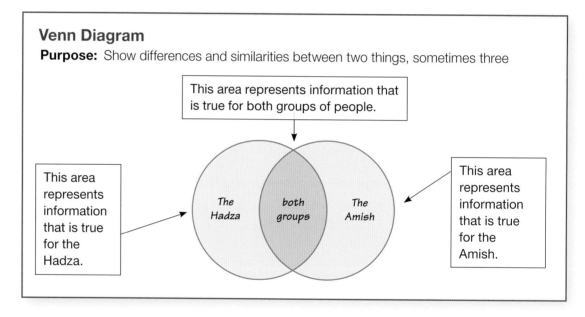

This area represents information that is true for both groups of people.

This area represents information that is true for the Hadza.

This area represents information that is true for the Amish.

The Hadza | both groups | The Amish

## Family Tree

**Purpose:** Organize information about your family relationships

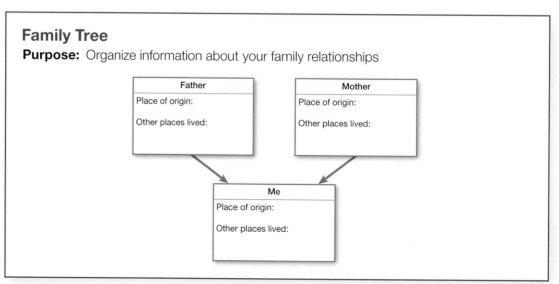

Father
Place of origin:
Other places lived:

Mother
Place of origin:
Other places lived:

Me
Place of origin:
Other places lived:

## Flow Chart

**Purpose:** Show the stages in a process, or a cause-and-effect chain  (Flow charts have many different shapes.)

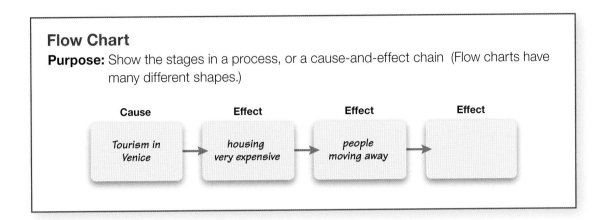

## Timeline

**Purpose:** Show the order of events and when they happened in time

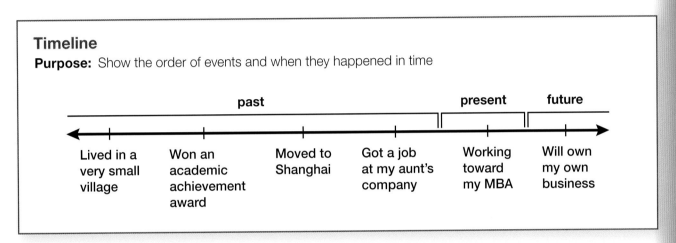

## Idea Map

**Purpose:** Brainstorm ideas or identify main points or themes of a listening or reading. (A Spider Map can also be used for this purpose.)

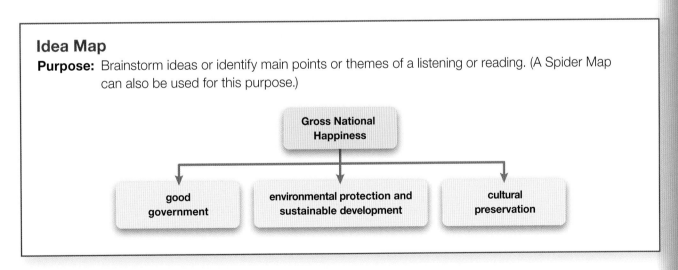

# Understanding and Using Visuals: Maps, Charts, Graphs, and Diagrams

**Maps** are used to show geographical information.

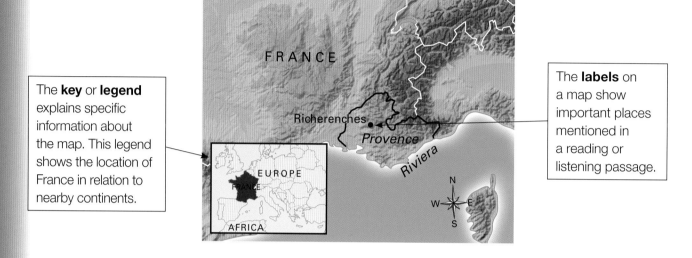

The **key** or **legend** explains specific information about the map. This legend shows the location of France in relation to nearby continents.

The **labels** on a map show important places mentioned in a reading or listening passage.

**Bar** and **line graphs** use axes to show the relationship between two or more things.

**Bar graphs** compare amounts and numbers.

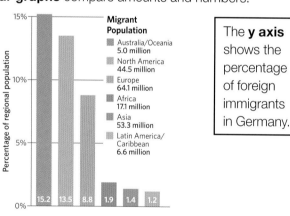

**Line graphs** show a change over time.

The **y axis** shows the percentage of foreign immigrants in Germany.

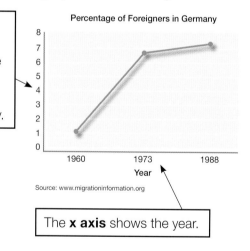

Percentage of Foreigners in Germany

Source: www.migrationinformation.org

The **x axis** shows the year.

**Pie charts** show percents of a whole, or something that is made up of several parts.

## Fossil Fuel Use by Sector

This section shows that the Energy Supply sector uses the most fossil fuels.

Waste and Wastewater 3%

Energy Supply 26%

Forestry 17%

Agriculture 14%

Industry 19%

Transportation 13%

Residential and Commercial Buildings 8%

**Diagrams** are a helpful way to show how a process or system works.

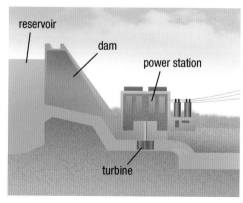

# Presentation Outline

When you are planning a presentation, you may find it helpful to use an outline. If it is a group presentation, the outline can provide an easy way to divide the content. For example, someone could do the introduction, another student the first main idea in the body, and so on.

I. **Introduction**

Topic: _____

_____

Hook/attention getter: _____

_____

Thesis statement: _____

_____

II. **Body**

A. First step/example/reason: _____

Supporting details:

1. _____
2. _____
3. _____

B. Second step/example/reason: _____

Supporting details:

1. _____
2. _____
3. _____

C. Third step/example/reason: _____

Supporting details:

1. _____
2. _____
3. _____

III. **Conclusion**

Major points to summarize: _____

_____

Any implications/suggestions/predictions: _____

_____

Closing comment/summary: _____

_____

# Checklists

## Research Checklist

- ☐ Do I have three to five sources for information in general—and especially for information I'm using without a specific citation?
- ☐ Am I correctly citing information when it comes from just one or two sources?
- ☐ Have I noted all sources properly, including page numbers?
- ☐ When I am not citing a source directly, am I using adequate paraphrasing? (a combination of synonyms, different word forms, and/or different grammatical structure)
- ☐ Are my sources reliable?

## Presentation Checklist

- ☐ Have I practiced several times?
- ☐ Did I get feedback from a peer?
- ☐ Have I timed the presentation?
- ☐ Do I introduce myself?
- ☐ Do I maintain eye contact?
- ☐ Do I explain my visuals?
- ☐ Do I pause sometimes and check for understanding?
- ☐ Do I use correct pronunciation?
- ☐ Do I have good posture?
- ☐ Am I using appropriate voice volume so that everyone can hear?

## Pair and Group Work Checklist

- ☐ Do I make eye contact with others?
- ☐ Do I pay attention when someone else is talking?
- ☐ Do I make encouraging comments?
- ☐ Do I ask for clarification when I don't understand something?
- ☐ Do I check for understanding?
- ☐ Do I clarify what I mean?
- ☐ Do I express agreement and disagreement politely?
- ☐ Do I make suggestions when helpful?
- ☐ Do I participate as much as my classmates?
- ☐ Do I ask my classmates for their ideas?

# Summary of Signal Phrases

**Giving Recommendations:**
*It's (probably) a good idea (not) to . . .*
*It might be wise (not) to . . .*
*If I were you, I wouldn't . . .*
*Have you thought about . . .?*

**Showing Understanding:**
*You must be (tired).*
*You must have been (glad).*
*That must be (fun).*
*That must have been (difficult).*

**Using Fillers:**
*Let me think*
*Just a moment*
*Oh, what's the word . . .*
*. . . um . . .*
*. . . hang on . . .*

**Expressing Uncertainty:**
*It appears/looks/seems as though . . .*
*It appears/seems to me (that) . . .*
*I'm not quite/altogether sure (that) . . .*
*I could be wrong, but it appears/doesn't*
    *appear (that) . . .*

**Paraphrasing:**
*I mean . . .*
*In other words . . .*
*That is (to say) . . .*
*Let me put it another way . . .*
*To put it another way . . .*

**Enumerating Reasons and Examples:**
*First, Second, Third . . .*
*First, Next, After that . . .*
*First, Then, And then . . .*
*For one thing, For another, And for*
    *another . . .*
*In the first place, In the second place,*
    *And in the third place . . .*

**Expressing a Lack of Knowledge:**
*I had no idea (that) . . .*
*I didn't realize (that) . . .*
*I never knew (that) . . .*
*I wasn't aware (that) . . .*

**Giving Effects or Results:**
*As a result, . . .*
*One consequence is . . .*
*Consequently . . .*
*Therefore, . . .*
*Another effect is . . .*

**Giving Definitions:**
*. . . which means . . .*
*In other words, . . .*
*What that means is . . .*
*Another way to say that is . . .*
*That is . . .*

**Expressing Opinions:**
*As far as I'm concerned, . . .*
*In my opinion, . . .*
*(Personally,) I think . . .*
*If you ask me, . . .*
*As I see it, . . .*

**Signal to Stop Taking Notes:**
*You don't have to write all this down . . .*
*This information is in your book . . .*
*You can find this in your handout . . .*
*This won't be on your test . . .*

**Returning to a Previous Topic:**
*So, just to restate . . .*
*Back to . . .*
*Getting back to what we were saying . . .*
*To return to what we were talking about*
    *earlier . . .*
*OK, so to get back on topic . . .*

**Understanding Sidetracks:**
*That reminds me . . .*
*By the way . . .*
*This is off the subject, but . . .*
*As an aside . . .*
*On a different topic . . .*

**Confirming Understanding:**
*Are you following me?*
*Does that make sense?*
*Have you got that?*
*Any questions?*
*Are you with me?*
*OK so far?*

# VOCABULARY INDEX

\*These words are on the Academic Word List (AWL). The AWL is a list of the 570 highest-frequency academic word families that regularly appear in academic texts. The AWL was compiled by researcher Averil Coxhead based on her analysis of a 3.5 million word corpus (Coxhead, 200).

## Critical Thinking

analyzing information, 101, 102–103, 121, 122–123, 129, 133, 141, 142–143, 161, 162–163, 167, 173, 181, 182–183, 187, 193, 195

asking questions for further research, 145

brainstorming, 113, 171, 185, 186

comparisons, 166

creating effective visuals, 200

debates, 191

distinguishing between relevant and irrelevant information, 207

evaluating a lawsuit, 150

evaluating numbers and statistics, 116

evaluating Web sources, 120

expressing and explaining opinions, 115, 129, 131, 153, 168, 185

identifying lecture topic, 202

making inferences, 173, 205

meaning from context, 104, 112, 124, 134, 144, 174, 184, 186–187, 194, 204

memory building, 180

note-taking using an outline, 206

organizing ideas, 171

predicting content, 106, 146, 166, 192, 202

proposing solutions for problems, 151, 197

questioning results, 167

recognizing a return to a previous topic, 207

recognizing speaker's bias, 205

recognizing speaker's organization, 206

relating content to personal experiences, 147

relating to personal opinion, 107, 113

remaining objective, 185

restating content, 131

summarizing, 127, 189, 206

supporting ideas, 168

understanding and using visuals/graphic organizers, 206
  charts, 122–123, 160, 171, 186, 196, 216
  diagrams, 216
  flow charts, 215
  graphs, 130, 216
  idea maps, 107, 215
  maps, 216
  T-charts, 214
  timelines, 215
  Venn diagrams, 214

understanding buzzwords, 109

understanding structure of presentation, 202–203

using new grammar, 110, 119, 129–130, 139, 149–150, 159, 170, 179, 189–190, 199

using new vocabulary, 105, 125, 135, 145, 155, 175

using notes, 207

## Grammar

connectors
  to add and emphasize information, 129–130
  of concession, 139
present participle phrases, 179
verbs
  causative, 189–190
  phrasal, 149–150
  subject-verb agreement with quantifiers, 170
  subjunctive, in *that* clauses, 199
  three-word phrasal, 159
  verb + gerund, 110
  verb + object + infinitive, 119

## Language Function. *See also* Grammar; Pronunciation; Speaking

agreeing or disagreeing, 210
apologizing for interrupting, 210
asking for clarification, 210
asking sensitive questions, 131, 210
asking who will go first, 151
checking background knowledge, 178, 211
conceding a point, 210
confirming understanding, 188–189, 219
congratulating the group, 107, 210
digressing from the topic, 138, 210
enumerating, 168–169, 211, 219
expressing approval and disapproval, 211
expressing encouragement, 210
expressing hopes, 210
expressing interest, 210
expressing lack of knowledge, 118, 219
expressing surprise, 210
expressing uncertainty, 148–149, 219
fillers, 108–109, 219
giving definitions, 219
giving effects or results, 219
giving recommendations, 198
joining a group, 171, 211
paraphrasing, 219
returning to a previous topic, 219
showing that you are following a conversation, 128–129
showing understanding, 158–159, 219
signals to stop taking notes, 219
understanding sidetracks, 219
using gestures, 171